CHRISTIANITY
IN AN AGE OF TERRORISM

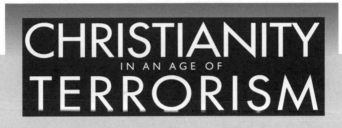

CHRISTIANITY
IN AN AGE OF
TERRORISM

GENE EDWARD VEITH

CONCORDIA PUBLISHING HOUSE · SAINT LOUIS

Dedicated to Rev. Larry Myers, a chaplain in the United States Air Force, who was in the Pentagon when the plane hit; and to Rev. Dean Kavouras, a chaplain in the Federal Bureau of Investigation, who was at the crash site in Pennsylvania. They both brought Christ to the survivors and the rescue workers.

Scripture taken from the HOLY BIBLE, NEW INTERNATIONAL VERSION®. NIV®. Copyright © 1973, 1978, 1984 by International Bible Society. Used by permission of Zondervan Publishing House. All rights reserved.

Copyright © 2002 by Gene Edward Veith
Published by Concordia Publishing House
3558 S. Jefferson Avenue, St. Louis, MO 63118-3968
Manufactured in the United States of America.

2 3 4 5 6 7 8 9 10   11 10 09 08 07 06 05 04 03 02

CONTENTS

PREFACE

I was asked to write this book by some friends at Concordia Publishing House. It was put together in just a little over a month and was finished on the six-month anniversary of the attack on New York, Pennsylvania, and Washington, D.C. What it lacks in polish, I hope it makes up for in intensity.

Some of the material in this book first appeared in my weekly columns for *World Magazine*. My colleagues at *World* are generous in granting permissions, asking only that those who reprint articles include information on how to subscribe: call 1-800-951-6397. There is also some material that first appeared in *The Lutheran Witness*.

Thanks go to Robert Knox and Paul McCain for initiating this project, also to Fred Baue for helping me see it through to completion. I thank Concordia University Wisconsin not only for supporting my work, but for providing laptop computers for faculty members, thus enabling me to work on this project night and day—while traveling, watching television, and waiting long hours in airports—which we travelers have to do since September 11. I also want to salute the students in my Tuesday classes; together we shared the experience of watching the towers fall down. I appreciate my brother-in-law, Paul Smith, who had relatives doing rescue work at the World Trade Center. Also, thanks go to my daughter Joanna, who works at the Naval Academy, where she had to help arrange a memorial service for one of their alumni, the pilot of one of the hijacked planes. All of this helped make it all seem real, as did the two chaplains whom I happened to know and to whom this book is dedicated. The prayer services that week at First Immanuel Lutheran Church in Cedarburg, Wisconsin, led by my pastor, Rev. Randall Raasch, helped me realize just how powerful Lutheran theology is when addressing the emotions, uncertainties, and responsibilities that arise in a time of national crisis. And I also want to thank my wife, Jackquelyn, for all of her help, support, and inspiration.

March 11, 2002

CHRISTIANITY
IN AN AGE OF TERRORISM

1

"Everything Has Changed"

We were going about our business pursuing what Francis Schaeffer considered the only values we had left: personal peace and affluence. Suddenly an airplane—and then another—flew into that great monument to American affluence, the World Trade Center in New York City. Soon after, another plane flew into the nerve center that protects American peace, the Pentagon. Then another plane crashed into the Pennsylvania heartland. Before long the economy went into a swoon, and the affluence Americans had taken for granted was shaken. Soon we were at war, and the peace Americans had taken for granted was gone.

Not just the lack of war, but *personal peace*—the old feeling of security—gave way to nervousness, even terror. Law-abiding Americans got the suspected-criminal treatment at airports, complete with warrant-less searches and even up-against-the-wall pat-downs. Everyday activities—a trip to the mall, an afternoon at the ball game, going to work—could be occasions for a suicide bomber setting himself off in a crowd. Even something as mundane as checking the mail now entailed the risk of an anthrax attack.

Long after the attack the global repercussions linger. Palestinians send teenage girls with explosives under their coats as human bombs to kill Israelis, who send tanks to bulldoze Palestinian houses. The Church of the Nativity in Bethlehem becomes the site of a bloody shoot-out—the place of Christ's birth profaned by blood shed in the name of hatred. It seems as if the world were coming apart, as if there is no solution to the escalating cycles of violence. In this new age of terrorism, there is no clear "exit strategy," no end in sight to the dangers and the insecurity.

Americans have lost their complacency. But this is not completely a bad thing. It is healthy to confront death and the ever present possibility of death. Besides, the nation is feeling emotions that seem strangely wholesome for people that had become jaded and cynical. Those who had loved ones killed in the attacks were filled with sorrow, but so were those who did not know anyone who died. People who had tended to be isolated and indifferent, minding their own business, who could care less about their neighbors, suddenly were feeling empathy, both for the victims and the bereaved.

Americans felt other emotions that they had not felt for a while: anger, fueled not by selfishness but by righteous indignation; and patriotism, even on the part of those who before had been cynical or dismissive of their country. A country that had been divided sometimes bitterly and sometimes just by the fact of its own pluralism came together in a genuine sense of national unity. The vocations that protect our society—police officers, firefighters, the military—callings that had earlier been targets of scathing criticism or condescension, now were seen as heroic.

It was not just the way people felt that was challenged, but the way they thought. What we experience as truth, said our intellectuals, is a construction, whether of the culture or the individual's own choices. The pop culture and even the conversations of ordinary folks reflected this postmodern relativism: "Truth is relative." "You construct your own reality." "That may be true for you, but it isn't true for me." But were the hijacked planes that crashed into those buildings—and into the consciousness of every American—"constructions"? Were the death and twisted metal and collapsed skyscrapers truths that were "relative"? Or was this all a traumatic example of objective reality that breaks in, oblivious to our subjectivity?

Moral values, too, had been assumed to be subjective, nothing more than social constructions, cultural preferences, or personal choices. Here, though, was a moral outrage in which the objectivity of right and wrong could be perceived with certain clarity. Those who took so many lives were—and the unfamiliar word was used over and over again—"evil." Conversely, those who gave their lives to rescue others were "good." From the courage of the passengers over Pennsylvania who resisted their hijackers, saving untold lives at the expense of their own, to the perfidy of Osama bin Laden and the treachery of John Walker Lindh—objective moral categories were thrown into high relief. The dogmas of cultural relativism could no longer excuse the tyranny of the Taliban. It appeared that there were absolutes, after all.

Of course, the immediate impact of 9-11—a date that ironically recalls the telephone number for emergencies—faded, at least somewhat. Lots of things went back to normal. When it happened, there was a spike in church attendance, but after a few weeks the number of churchgoers returned to normal. There was a surge of volunteers to charities right after the attacks, but only a fraction of those eager volunteers actually showed up. The entertainment industry shut down the week of the attack, but not for long. The war against the al Qaeda terrorists in Afghanistan produced easy early results, not demanding much sacrifice after all, though Americans would have been glad to give it. A plan to erect a statue to honor the firefighters who raised a flag at ground zero degenerated into the same old racial divisiveness. Partisan bickering started up again. The pursuit of personal peace and affluence resumed.

And yet, the events of September 11, 2001, remain a watershed moment for American culture. They linger. Despite rapid progress in Afghanistan, the war with terrorism continues. Americans are not the way they were. Our history has gone into another phase. People are saying, "Everything has changed."

Those who study the great epochs of Western culture have often used the destruction of buildings as signposts of a new era.[1] The modern era began, say some cultural historians, with the destruction of the Bastille, the French prison, on July 14, 1789. The Enlightenment revolution overthrew tradition, authority, and faith, all in an effort to create from scratch a new utopian order of reason and humanism, a mindset that would dominate Western culture, through numerous reigns of terror, for two centuries. The modernist attempt to solve all social ills through humanistic assumptions and scientific rationalism resulted not in a utopia, but in crime, degradation, and despair. This modern era had its symbolic ending with the demolition of another building, marking the beginning of the postmodern era. On July 15, 1972, the Pruitt-Igoe housing project in St. Louis—confidently designed to better the lot of the poor through social engineering—was purposely blown up.

If the fall of great works of architecture are milestones for cultural change, then surely the collapse of the World Trade Center—twin towers of 110 stories utterly destroyed by a terrorist attack—marks the end of postmodernism and the beginning of something new.

What is next? Despite the passage of time, the dust has not yet settled so that we can see clearly where we are now.

Confusion is rampant. Here we are, a high-tech, advanced civilization facing an enemy right out of the Dark Ages. We are nice people, we have always assumed. Why do they hate us?

Even though we live in a modern secular state and

even though a good percentage of Americans are not particularly religious, we find ourselves in a religious war. The historic struggle between Islam and Christianity seems anachronistic, especially for secularists who have no interest in the contending theologies but are still treated as targets.

Christians find themselves in a precarious position. While they believe the kingdom of heaven comes through evangelism, not jihad, their own culture may be turning against them. As noted by some of our leading thinkers, the evil of the Islamic terrorists consists of religious extremism. The only solution to the holy-war mentality and to the Taliban assaults on human freedom is religious tolerance. In our country we also have religious extremists—those Christians who believe they have the only way to salvation, who believe in imposing their morality on others, or who oppose a woman's right to abortion and the sick person's right to die. There is no essential difference, they say, between an Islamic conservative and a Christian conservative. A comprehensive war against terrorism must stamp them both out.

This might entail a new hypersecularism, in which the state and the culture turn completely against religion of any kind, seeing in every spiritual belief the shadow of a potential terrorist.

Or it might entail a new religion entirely. Before September 11 the watchword was *diversity* and tolerance meant respecting the rights of other people to be different. After September 11 the watchword is *unity.* Tolerance is being redefined as the insistence that everyone is really the same. In the aftermath of the tragic attacks, Americans joined in interfaith services, in which Christians, Jews, Hindus, Buddhists, Sikhs, and Muslims joined together for prayer and worship. Certainly it was in the interest of the United States government to convey the message that our war effort is "not against Islam," so Muslims were given prominent place, their faith honored as "a religion of peace." It was certainly understandable that the president would call for the prayers of people of all faiths. But the events played into the hands of the theologians who once had worked for the unity of all Christians and are now working for the unity of all world religions. The interfaith movement teaches that, whatever our religion, we all pray to the same God and each religious path leads to the same goal. Though not everyone who participated in these services intended to convey that message, and, in fact, many were motivated by the possibility of evangelism, in truth it is evangelism that the interfaith movement would outlaw.

In his book *The Spiritual Society*, written well before the September 11 attacks, Frederic W. Baue argues that what will succeed postmodernism is a new religious consciousness. This spiritual society, though, will have a new religion grounded in syncretism, a combination of various faiths. Along with the belief that all religions are equally valid, the new syncretic religion will reject—and possibly even persecute— faiths that are not "inclusive." This will prove a problem for those whose Scriptures teach that "all the gods of the nations are idols" (Psalm 96:5), and who believe in

Jesus, who said, "I am the way and the truth and the life. No one comes to the Father except through Me" (John 14:6).

Christians are facing other issues in this new cultural climate. Questions of citizenship—what do I owe Christ, and what do I owe my country—are more urgent than ever. Might they conflict? Yet what about this deep sense of patriotism that I do, in fact, feel? Is love of country idolatrous, sinful, or dangerous?

What about war? What a strange war this is, with hidden terrorists trying to kill not soldiers but ordinary civilians. Our own military is armed with the latest technology, making it so very lethal. How do the old tenets of the "just war" apply to terrorism, and can a Christian, in good conscience, be a combatant?

What about Islam? Why has it been growing so quickly, and what is its allure? Is it really, at least in its moral teachings, the same as Christianity? How is Christianity different from all other world religions? How can we be tolerant in a pluralistic society without falling into syncretism?

If we are in a new cultural era, the church will face new temptations and will find new opportunities for the proclamation of the Gospel. The Word of God, of course, abides forever (1 Peter 1:25). The answers to these questions can be found in Scripture and in the confessions of the church, which are drawn from Scripture. These teachings, grounded in history, can guide us through these tumultuous and uncertain times.

NOTE TO CHAPTER 1

1. See Thomas Oden, in *Two Worlds: Notes on the Death of Modernity in America and Russia* (Downers Grove, IL: Inter-Varsity Press, 1992), p. 32, and Charles Jencks, *The Language of Post-Modern Architecture* (London: Academy Editions, 1984), p. 9. Oden sees the fall of the Berlin Wall as marking the end of modernism and the beginning of postmodernism. See also my book *Postmodern Times: A Christian Guide to Contemporary Thought and Culture* (Wheaton, IL: Crossway Books, 1994), pp. 27–46.

2

THE CROSS AT GROUND ZERO

Horrific disasters and any kind of suffering on a monumental scale inevitably raise the question, Where was God? This was certainly the case after the terrorists attacked the World Trade Center, the Pentagon, and the plane over Pennsylvania. Interestingly, such questions do not tend to be raised at the time or immediately thereafter. In the immediate aftermath of devastation, when the suffering is still raw—these are times of prayer, not doubt. People in their anguish turn to God, and in times like those He seems particularly real.

This was certainly the case on 9-11 and the days that followed. People prayed and asked for prayers. Even hardened reporters covering that story on the scene, for all of their liberal and secular bias, ended their interviews with survivors with remarks to the effect that "our prayers are with you," an invocation of faith seldom heard over the airwaves. Schools reportedly suspended their rule against prayer in school as teachers and students alike who watched the replays of the plane crashing into the tower could do nothing else but pray. The president formally called for a national day of prayer. Churches across America gladly complied and were packed with citizens holding candles, praying for their country and their fellow Americans. On the Capitol steps, lawmakers of both parties joined in a song that was very much a prayer, "God bless America," a song that reverberated at sporting events and public gatherings throughout the nation.

Later, though, after the tumultuous emotions died down, some took the occasion to ask how a loving God could have sat by to watch this happen. Sometimes this was in the context of wanting to blame the whole event on religion. Some pundits, no less than some ecumenical theologians, insisted that there is no difference between the religious zealots who committed the suicide mass murders and the religious folks who turned to God in their churches. For them, the question, Where was God? was a way of saying that there is no such thing. For others, especially those stricken with grief at the death of their loved ones, the question was an attempt to understand the meaning of what had happen. It is indeed a legitimate question.

Again, for some people the answer is that God was absent. Perhaps there is no God at all, as the atheists have always insisted. Or, God is as helpless as the rest of us, as in the theodicy of Rabbi Kushner's best-selling book *When Bad Things Happen to Good People.* Then there are the glibly sentimental Openness of God theologians, who teach that God is not omniscient or omnipotent. He is a deity, but more like us, with limited powers, who was presumably as surprised as the rest of us at what happened.

Others believed that God was on those airplanes, crashing into the symbols of American prosperity and power, in an act of divine judgment. This was the view of the terrorists. They were acting in the name of Allah. They considered themselves martyrs for the true faith, going so far as to wash themselves, adorn their bodies, and pray to prepare themselves for their holy death. America, they believed, is populated with infidels, filled with sin and decadence and oppression against the Muslim people of the world. America, in their cosmology, is the Great Satan. So to die—and kill—in a great act of retribution is a good work, to be rewarded eternally in Paradise. God was with them, the terrorists sincerely believed. Ironically, some Christian leaders, in some ill-considered but spontaneous opinions, believed pretty much the same thing. They assumed that in the attacks God was punishing America for our tolerance of abortion, homosexuality, and other sins. Not that they supported the terrorist attacks—and they quickly backtracked over the insensitive timing and effect of their remarks—but they interpreted the horrors of that day in terms of God's wrath. God was on the outside, looking down on New York, Washington, and Pennsylvania, throwing His thunderbolts.

But surely the best answer was given by one of the survivors, who worked on an upper story of the World Trade Center and who had to evacuate the building by crowding into a dark, smoke-filled stairway and going down countless flights of steps before the tower collapsed. He said that in the faces of the rescue workers—who were fighting their way *up* the stairs, trying to save those who were trapped, only to lose their own lives when the towers fell—he could see the face of God.

GOD IN VOCATION

The rescue workers, the firefighters and police officers who survived, were not used to the acclaim they suddenly received. "We were just doing our jobs," they said—with the same words used by World War II veterans. And yet, their dogged work round the clock in the hopes of finding survivors, their continuous labor for weeks and months at ground zero recovering remains and honoring the dead—this must have been motivated by something. Perhaps they, in turn, saw the face of God in the shocked, dust-covered faces of survivors or in the faces of the dead they pulled out of the rubble.

This is the biblical understanding of the presence of God. He indeed is in heaven where He reigns as king and judge over the whole universe, but—in the vast divide that separates Christianity from other religions such as Islam—He came into the world that He made by becoming incarnate in Jesus Christ. And Christ drained the cup of human suffering by bearing all sin and dying on the cross. He rose from the dead and ascended into heaven, but He is still present in His Word and His Sacraments. His presence in the church and in the hearts of those who believe in Him is real and actual. But He is also present in the world.

Jesus is present in one's neighbor—in particular, the suffering neighbor. "I was hungry and you gave Me something to eat, I was thirsty and you gave Me something to drink, I was a stranger and you invited Me in, I needed clothes and you clothed Me, I was sick and you looked after Me, I was in prison and you came to visit Me" (Matthew 25:35–36). When did we do any of this? "I tell you the truth, whatever you did for one of the least of these brothers of Mine, you did for Me" (Matthew 25:40).

The comment by rescue workers about "just doing their jobs" points to another facet of God's presence in the world. He is present in human vocations.[1]

When we pray the Lord's Prayer, said Luther, we ask God to give us our daily bread. He does give us our daily bread, and He does so through the work—the vocation—of the farmer and the baker. We might add the truck driver, the grocery store workers, the kid at the fast-food outlet, the bankers that finance it all, and every player in the economic system that puts on our table the food we need to live. It is still God who gives us our daily bread, but, while He could indeed feed us with heavenly manna, He chooses to work through means, through human beings "just doing their jobs."

The purpose of vocation is to love and serve one's neighbor in the various ways that are needed. God calls individuals, through their unique gifts and interests and opportunities, into distinct "offices," each with its unique authorities and prerogatives. Each Christian has a calling in the church, in the family, as a worker, and as a citizen.

The doctrine of vocation is one of the great theological contributions of the Reformation. God brings new life in the world through parents, heals through the medical professions, teaches through teachers, and protects—and rescues—people through police officers and firefighters. He literally was present in those rescue workers rushing up the stairs of the World Trade Center.

A key text for the doctrine of vocation is the Bible's description of how God restrains evil through earthly authorities:

> Everyone must submit himself to the governing authorities, for there is no authority except that which God has established. The authorities that exist have been established by God. Consequently, he who rebels against the authority is rebelling against what God has instituted, and those who do so will bring judgment on themselves. For rulers hold no terror for those who do right, but for those who do wrong. Do you want to be free from fear of the one who is in authority? Then do what is right, and he will commend you. For he is God's servant to do you good. But if you do wrong, be afraid, for he does not bear the sword for nothing. He is God's servant, an agent of wrath to bring punishment on the wrongdoer. Therefore, it is necessary to submit to the authorities, not only because of possible punishment but also because of conscience. This is also why you pay taxes, for the authorities are God's servants. (Romans 13:1–6)

The first use of God's moral Law is to restrain human sinfulness, if only externally, so that civil society will be possible. God, the only intrinsic authority, invests human beings with some of His authority. In the governing vocations, God is at work. The ruler, for all of his rank, is nothing more than "God's servant." He is a "minister," one through whom God works, to punish wrongdoing and to protect those who do right.

This applies specifically to those who "bear the sword"—police officers, presidents, and the military. Right before this chapter, St. Paul tells Christians, "Do not take revenge, my friends, but leave room for God's wrath, for it is written: 'It is Mine to avenge; I will repay,' says the Lord" (Romans 12:19). In this chapter St. Paul tells how the Lord wreaks that vengeance: through specific vocations that are given that responsibility. While Christians are told that it is wrong for individuals to take revenge, they are assured that the lawful official is "an agent of wrath to bring punishment on the wrongdoer" (Romans 13:4).

These are strong words, hard for us to accept. Does this mean that the governing status quo is always right? No. Not all rulers punish evil and protect their people. Some oppress their people instead of protecting them. Some seize power to promote their own selfish and evil projects. Some who have seized power lack all legal legitimacy. No one elected the Taliban, who ousted the legally constituted Afghan government and imposed their brutal, oppressive laws on a terrorized people. The Islamic students who took it upon themselves to whip unveiled women and people engaged in innocent pleasures such as music or kite flying and who hanged transgressors at the soccer field had no authority to do that. They were acting outside their vocation. Romans 13 does not sanction tyrants—who in tyrannizing their neighbors instead of protecting them are likewise acting outside their vocation—nor does it mean citizens may not criticize their rulers. In fact, under a democratic republic such as the United States, the people choose their own rulers, so that citizens are not only subjects but are themselves the ultimate rulers.

At any rate, Romans 13 has gained a new resonance in the aftermath of the attacks and the war against terrorism. The president—in an office that had fallen into some disrespect—has risen in stature and popularity, as he carries out his vocation as "God's servant to do [us] good." More than that, he is bearing the sword to "bring punishment on the wrongdoer." We are not used to war, but the actions of the army, navy, marines, and air force—again, individuals with a special vocation and authority to protect their neighbors by fighting the enemies who would harm them—have rallied the nation. With their laser-directed precision bombs, their daisy cutters, and their daring raids, they have indeed become "a terror" to the terrorists. They and the president and the law-enforcement agencies remain under God's Law, and they must not abuse their power, something citizens must be vigilant against. But, yes, God is present in the vocation of those who bear the sword.

The doctrine of vocation means that God is at work not just in His spiritual kingdom—manifested in the church and lasting into eternal life—but also in the world. God is active even in those who are not Christians, working through the vocation of nonbelieving farmers to feed the just and the unjust, rescuing people through nonbelieving rescue workers, punishing evil through secular-minded officials and servicemen who bear the sword. God has two kingdoms, the spiritual and the secular, and Christians are citizens of both. This is why Christians are to be involved in their nations and their culture, why they have vocations of citizenship.

This is why Christians can love their country. God rules, even among those who do not acknowledge Him. His sovereignty is not something that must be established, as if we needed to "win the world for Christ" or elect Christians to every public office in order to implement God's kingdom. Rather, God's sovereignty is already an existing fact. True, this world is a battleground between God and the devil, between civic virtue and sin, Law and lawlessness. Nevertheless, God reigns, and He does so through lawful institutions and valid vocations.

Christians, however, know that earthly institutions will always be tainted by sin, that they will never attain perfection. Understanding the distinction between God's two kingdoms means that the earthly realm must never be swallowed up by the spiritual realm. Nor may the spiritual realm be swallowed up by the earthly realm. In either case, the result would be a divinized state and a this-worldly religion. The purpose of the church is not to rule society; its message is not political; its goal is not social reform. To be sure, the church must proclaim God's Law, which means it will exert a moral influence on the society as a whole. But it is not the Law that constitutes the church. It is the Gospel. The church has to be, at essence, not of this world—saving people out of a world that is passing away into the life that never ends.

Ironically, it is the belief in a utopia—the various dreams of some divinized state or a this-worldly religion—that breeds terrorists. Those who believe that life on earth and social institutions are perfectible are always the destroyers. Indeed, the obviously imperfect status quo must be demolished in order to create something better. And since evil is what they think they are destroying in the name of a good purpose, they are oblivious to their own evil, seeing themselves as righteous and justified no matter how many people they murder. This is true of those terrorists who were Communists, assassinating the bourgeoisie so as to usher in the workers' paradise, and it is true of those terrorists who were fascists, who killed and blew up whatever stood in the way of their spiritualized state. To this day, left-wing terrorists and right-wing terrorists are utopians, striking their blows in the name of their idealized social order. And it is particularly true of Islamic terrorists, for whom there is no distinction between a spiritual and an earthly kingdom, whose religious purpose is not the salvation of souls but the imposition of Islamic law and the establishment of an Islamic state.

Today's terrorist attacks throw vocation into high relief. Part of the horror is how they turn vocation upside down. It is the vocation of our servicemen to fight—even to die—for their country. It is an office they assume on behalf of and in the stead of the rest of us civilians, loving and serving their neighbors by protecting them from their enemies. Terrorists, though, try to avoid fighting the military; instead, they strive to fight and kill civilians. In a terrorist war, civilians, not soldiers, are the major casualties. Conversely, in the current war against terrorism, waged by our military, the whole nation of Afghanistan—a land notoriously resistant to conquest from the time of Alexander the Great to the time of the Soviet Union—was for the most part taken in a few short weeks, yet hardly any servicemen were killed. A few were taken by enemy fire; a CIA agent was murdered by a prisoner uprising; some others were killed by accidents—sad and noble sacrifices to be sure, but astonishingly, blessedly few. And yet America suffered some 3,000 dead at the hands of the enemy, nearly all—with the exception of some military workers at the Pentagon—ordinary citizens whose calling was to work in an office, fly an airplane, take care of their children, rescue the injured, or put out fires. They did not have the vocation or the expectation that they would die for their country at the hands of their nation's enemies, and yet they did.

Another odd confusion of vocation came when al Qaeda captives were imprisoned at Guantanamo Bay in Cuba. Keeping them in cages and subduing them with shackles and hoods is a violation of international law, some critics insisted. The Geneva Conventions set forth how prisoners of war are to be treated. Those accords do regulate the treatment of captured military forces. Besides not having to give any more information than their "name, rank, and serial number," captured soldiers must not be treated like criminals. They must retain the privileges of their ranks and be housed in barracks roughly equivalent to the way the conquering forces are housed. They are even to get their military pay. After the war is over, they must be sent back home. The Geneva Conventions recognize that someone who kills in battle is not the same as a murderer. That is, they recognize that a soldier is acting in vocation.

But do the Geneva Conventions apply to al Qaeda terrorists? Are they soldiers, entitled to the military status of prisoners of war? Interestingly, the treaty specifically distinguishes between "lawful combatants," those who are entitled to its provisions, and "unlawful combatants," those who are not. For one thing, lawful combatants, according to the Geneva Conventions, must wear uniforms. Wearing a uniform distinguishes a soldier, who is acting under the authority of his government, from a civilian. That is, a uniform is a "robe of office," signifying a lawful vocation, just as a pastor's vestments or a judge's robes symbolize and express the special authority they are entitled to exercise.

Combatants in civilian clothes, with hidden weapons, creating mayhem against civilians in non-combat zones enjoy no protection under the laws of war. Spies, pirates, and terrorists are not POWs. Traditionally they could be summarily executed. Terrorists —unlike, say, our nation's enemies in the past, such as a German foot soldier or a Russian pilot or a North Vietnamese officer—do not have the "office" to wage war, lacking both a government to authorize their actions on its behalf and a lawful discipline to direct their combat against military targets.

Terrorism wreaks violence upon the very fabric of society. This includes violating vocation. And yet, in those targeted by terrorism, vocation can be seen all the more as a precious gift of God. Not only firefighters, police officers, and other rescue workers, but pilots and flight attendants and chaplains assumed a heroic cast in the September 11 assault. The office of the presidency and the man who occupied that office acquired a new grandeur. Airmen, marines, and special-forces fighters played their part. Examination of more humble callings, such as airport security personnel and baggage handlers, loomed in importance. Postal workers, medical personnel, and office workers—not just those who died but the rest of them who knew that the same thing could happen to them—became more significant. The most foundational vocation of them all, that of the family, was seen in a new light as husbands and wives, fathers and mothers, children and in-laws grieved in either loss or sympathy and clung closer to each other.

TERRORISM AND THE CROSS

Christians know that their God is the One who came down from heaven, put off His glory, and became one of us. More than that, He suffered at the hands of sinners and was tortured to death. And in God's humiliation, suffering, and death, He atoned for *our* sins. We find ourselves forgiven for the evil that is in us. And because He rose again from the dead, we have the assurance that we, too, will know the resurrection unto everlasting life.

As has often been noted, this is an odd way of salvation. Most religions—including Islam—stress what *we* must do. Christianity stresses what *God, in Christ,* has done for us. But even if God were to save us, we might expect a different way than the death of Christ on a cross. We might expect Him to stage a cosmic battle, a hand-to-hand combat with Satan, ending in the evil one's destruction. Or maybe God could come to earth as the great king that He is, subjugating earth to His perfect rule. And yet He defies all of our expectations. He comes not in glory, but in the cross. And He calls us not to glory but to bear crosses of our own (Matthew 16:24).

This distinction between what Luther called the theology of the cross and the theology of glory is critical in an age of terrorism. Not only is it comforting for those who will suffer as victims in these times, since the Christ who has borne the sins of the world also "took up our infirmities and carried our sorrows" (Isaiah 53:4). It is a realistic faith that recognizes hardship, frustration, and failure, transfiguring them with the grace of God. It also helps to distinguish between a distinctly Christian spirituality and what we are up against. Terrorists—whether religious or secular, left-wing or right-wing—invariably hold to a theology of glory.

They are convinced that by their actions they will build the kingdom of heaven on earth with their own hands. They are convinced that in all of their killings and bombings and terrorizing of the nonbelievers in their cause they are doing a great and noble work. Those who are religious have no doubt that they are glorifying their god and that he will glorify them, rewarding them richly for what they are doing for him. Suicide bombers imagine themselves to be martyrs and are hailed as such by their friends and families, lauded as earning eternal pleasures for their self-sacrifice in destroying the enemies of god. Communist and fascist terrorists, of course, do not think in terms of a god, but they see themselves as part of a great social movement that gives their lives and their actions in its behalf meaning and affirmation. Though they themselves may die gloriously for the cause, they are ushering in their utopias, and future generations will praise their names.

The theology of the cross, on the other hand, teaches that spirituality is not to be found in assertions of the self over against others, nor in seizing or demanding power, nor in the kind of pride and self-righteousness that excuses every cruelty toward those it deems lesser. The end of all theologies of glory—which can often arise even within Christianity—is the deification of the self. The cross means the humbling of the self in light of God's incarnation, His action, and His grace.

It is not that human beings must sacrifice themselves for God; He sacrifices Himself for human beings. It is not a matter of ascending up to Him; rather, He descends to us. God, in Christ, is present in the human condition.

He is hidden, to use another of Luther's images. When someone is hidden, he is present, just not seen. God hides Himself in unexpected ways and in unexpected places. He is hidden in the homeless child in the manger and in the despised carpenter executed as a criminal. Today, that Christ is hidden in His Word and Sacraments in an unassuming church service. He is hidden in human vocations. And He is hidden in human suffering.

In the wreckage of the World Trade Center, in which the girder-melting heat of burning jet fuel caused one of the tallest buildings in the world to collapse upon itself, nearly everything was crushed and incinerated beyond recognition. Sifting through the smoking rubble two days later, the rescue workers found a perfectly shaped cross standing almost upright, formed by the fusion of two metal girders. "Some people will say it's velocity or physics that put it there," said Frank Silecchia, who found the cross. "To me, it's an act of God." Those carrying out their vocations at ground zero moved the cross to a 40-foot tall foundation so that they all could see it as they went about their work. It was adopted by those toiling at the site, as the Associated Press quoted Silecchia, as "a symbol of hope, our symbol of faith, our symbol of healing."[2]

One need not venerate this cross, as some did, or even see it as a miracle as such, to recognize that this is the Christian answer to the question, Where is God amidst all of this horror? He is on the cross at ground zero—Golgotha, New York City, the hospital ward, every ground zero of human desolation. God is in Christ on the cross, reconciling the world to Himself.

NOTES TO CHAPTER 2

1. See Gustav Wingren, *Luther on Vocation* (Minneapolis: Fortress Press; reprint, Evansville, IN: Ballast Press, 1994). See also my book *God at Work: Your Christian Vocation in All of Life* (Wheaton, IL: Crossway Books, 2002).

2. Shannon McCaffrey, "Cast Iron 'Cross' Found in World Trade Center Rubble Gives Rescue Workers Hope," Associated Press, 5 October 2001.

3

HOLY WARS
MUSLIM AND CHRISTIAN

The most unsettling thing about terrorists may be their self-righteousness. They cold-bloodedly murder as many people as they can—children, women, and innocent bystanders; they set off explosions that destroy and maim; they steal and lie and deceive, financing their operations by credit-card fraud or even heroin dealing. And all the while they are utterly pious and moralistic. All of their cruelty is completely justified in their minds. They are serving their god. They are obeying their scriptures. Those who attach explosives to themselves, walk into pizza parlors or shopping malls, and set themselves off are not condemned by their fellow believers as suicide-murderers but rather hailed as martyrs for the faith. Their parents, interviewed on the news after another young man or woman commits a suicide-bombing, are thankful, expressing gratitude for the privilege of having raised a martyr.

What is this mind-set? Nothing seems more alien than the capacity to do such evil and yet—far from feeling guilt about what one has done—feel such moral superiority. That a mother would *want* her child to die a suicide and a murderer staggers the imagination.

What is true of Islamic radicals is also true of other terrorists. The coldhearted self-righteousness of Timothy J. McVeigh, the White Supremacists, the Peruvian communists known as the Shining Path, the Irish Republican Army, the Earth Liberation Front—all are motivated by an ideology that can justify the most horrible acts and leave those who commit them feeling exquisitely upright, moral, and good. The religious among them, such as the Islamic terrorists, are convinced that committing such atrocities is a means of salvation, making them acceptable to their god for martyring themselves or slaying his enemies.

Terrorists have a religious zeal and a religious motivation, but theirs is a religion of a particular kind, namely, an extreme brand of legalism. They think they are saved by their works. They follow what they construe as the law of their god with a single-minded virtue, even when this leads them to violate the moral Law of all religions.

Christians, too, can get this way—and often have in the sad saga of history—but the uniqueness of the Christian faith is its opposition to legalism. We are saved, Christians say, not by our works but by the grace of God in Jesus Christ. What makes Christians is not some moral exertion, but the exertion of Christ—the only moral man, who fulfilled the whole Law on our behalf; the Lamb of God, who atoned for our sins on the cross. Christianity is a religion of Gospel, not a religion of Law. Yes, Christians believe in God's moral Law, but they are conscious that what they need most is forgiveness for having broken that Law. They are motivated and enabled to keep that Law by their faith in what Christ has done for them and in the love that flows from that faith.

The great obstacle to faith is not sin. Sin can be forgiven, and acknowledging one's sin is what makes a person open to the Gospel. The great obstacle to faith and salvation is self-righteousness. Those who think they do not need God's grace, who imagine that they are doing fine as they are, who have such pride in their own goodness—these are the ones who shut out Christ. In His time on earth, prostitutes, tax-collectors, and sinners of every kind flocked to Him. He was opposed and later slain by the scribes and the Pharisees, who were complacent and smug in their own legalism. So it has been throughout history and today. Only the broken and penitent, those desperate in their inability to keep God's Law, grasp the Gospel and hold to Christ in faith. To the self-righteous, God's Law must be proclaimed in its full, radical intensity until they realize that they are not righteous at all in God's sight. Then, humbled and terrified by the Law of God, they will find Christ's promise of forgiveness good news indeed.

Some of those who are convinced of their righteousness, persisting in their exquisite feeling of their own goodness, become, ironically, some of the most vicious sinners. Religions can reinforce their egos, heightening their sense of moral superiority to other human beings. This shuts out love. The religiously self-righteous consider sinners with disgust. Blind to their own sinfulness, they apply the highest standards of judgment to others, though not themselves, and become quite willing to punish the infidel. God—or justice, or the cause—wills it. And because they are self-righteous, they feel no guilt despite the enormities of what they do to others.

The spirituality that gives rise to terrorism has two major components. One is legalism. The other is the theology of glory, as opposed to the theology of the cross described in the last chapter. This applies to all kinds of terrorism as found in all kinds of religions, including those, like communism and fascism, that have a secularist veneer. This chapter focuses on Islam, the religion involved in our current conflict, but the traits discussed here can be found in other religions, including Christianity, which has in its history terrorism of its own. The Christian church, too, has been guilty of legalism, forgetting the Gospel of Jesus Christ; it has often forgotten the cross to pursue instead its own glory. This has manifested itself in crusades, inquisitions, pogroms, and ethnic cleansing.

Nevertheless, the Christian church cannot for long remain itself apart from the Gospel and the cross. The Gospel, the Bible's central teaching, will keep reasserting itself as it did in the Reformation. Islam, however, is the supreme religion of Law. It is the supreme religion of glory.

THE FASTEST GROWING RELIGION

A few years ago a student came up to me during a break and started to talk. It was a night class in an adult education course. She, like so many others in the class, was a white, middle-class, single mom, living in the suburbs, holding a good job, but wanting to go back to school to finish her degree so she could climb up the ladder in her career. We had been discussing some work of literature (I forget now what it was), and we had been drawing out some of its moral and spiritual themes. I called a break, but she wanted to talk about it some more. She launched into her life story. Her life used to be really messed up, she said. She had been a rebellious teenager, was into drugs, got into some really bad relationships, but then, she said, her life changed when she—I thought she was going to say "discovered Jesus Christ," as in similar "testimonies" I have heard from students. Instead, she said her life changed when she discovered Islam. Now, she said, she has straightened out her moral life. Now she has order in her life. Now life has meaning. She was so happy, she just wanted to share her faith.

I realized then that Christianity was in for some competition. I had come to know many Muslim college students as a graduate student and as a professor. Many of them were not just Muslims but Islamic radicals. But the political issues they were obsessed with seemed distant. Many Muslims in the United States have been immigrants, bringing their faith with them from their homeland, enjoying the freedom of religion that is one of this nation's great legacies. For all of their hard work in pursuit of the American dream—I have always admired their diligence—their religion still seemed "foreign." Islam had also gained a strong foothold among African Americans, many of whom felt that Islam was more African than their "slave religion" of Christianity. (Never mind that Christianity was African since the time of the Ethiopian eunuch and St. Augustine, that Muslims converted their African holdings with the sword, and that it was Islamic slave traders who captured and sold Africans to the Americas.) Still, the Black Muslims in their suits and bow ties were at least doing good work in ridding neighborhoods of drug dealers and building strong "family values" among the poorest of the poor. But now, talking to this student, I saw Islam spreading into the American middle class.

Since then, Americans have had a different kind of confrontation with Islam. Muslim terrorists are angrily waging bloody jihad against Americans, who are bewildered as to why they hate us so much. Other Americans see all Muslims as the enemy, sometimes going so far as to mistreat honest Muslim citizens. But something else has happened. Since the attack on September 11, 2001, polls show that Islam has a higher approval rating than ever. More than that, the number of conversions to Islam has skyrocketed.

In the four months after September 11, some 34,000 Americans converted to Islam.[1] Islam is now the fastest growing religion in the United States. Of the six million Muslims in the United States, more than 30 percent of those who attend mosques are converts.[2] This is becoming a phenomenon in the Hispanic community, with some 25,000 converts in New York and California. Latino Muslims seem to see themselves as returning to the Moorish heritage of ancient Spain. There is a veritable Muslim revival taking place in the nation's prisons. In the state of New York, between 40 and 60 percent of black prisoners have converted to Islam.[3]

Those who became Muslims immediately after the attack, though, were largely affluent white Americans, particularly women. Journalist Gretchen Ertl interviewed a number of new post-9-11 converts, nearly all of them women. They told her that they by no means supported the acts of terrorism but that the press coverage Islam had received after the attack— including accounts of Muslims being mistreated and the perpetually trumpeted message that real Islam is a religion of peace—made them curious. They investigated the religion, met with Muslim clerics, and found themselves drawn in.

"I said the testimony [the confession that there is no God but Allah, and Mohammed is his prophet] and, poof, I was a Muslim," said Tiffany Motschenbacher, a 30-year-old theater major from Michigan. "I was shaking and weeping. I really felt that this religion was the truth and what I'd been looking for my whole life. I used to feel something was wrong with me because I couldn't grasp the concept of God. Now I finally had peace of heart."[4]

"Americans have bought more flags since 9/11, but they've also bought more Korans," said Imam Siraj Wahhaj, who heads a mosque in Brooklyn, not far from where the World Trade Center once stood. "I've had more converts since 9/11 and I've spoken in so many different forums and inter-faith meetings."[5]

The converts Ertl interviewed repudiated terrorism and insisted their newfound faith had nothing to do with the attacks on America. Other converts, of course, go to the radical side. Take John Walker Lindh, the American al Qaeda member captured in Afghanistan. Then there was Richard Reid, the English citizen who was thwarted from blowing up an airliner when he tried to light the bomb in his shoe. (Islam is growing in England and the rest of Europe even more rapidly than in the United States.) The chilling words of Osama bin Laden, captured on videotape, exult in the evangelistic effect of the 9-11 attacks: "In Holland, the number of people who accepted Islam during the days that followed the operations were more than the people who accepted Islam in the last 11 years. I heard someone on Islamic radio who owns a school in America say: 'We don't have time to keep up with the demands of those who are asking about Islamic books to learn about Islam.' This event made people think [about true Islam], which benefited Islam greatly."

What is the attraction? Why would someone embrace a religion that is so severe and demanding—especially those from a contemporary secular culture known for loose morality, self-indulgence, and freedom unbound? Islam forbids alcohol. As in the Old

Testament, pork and other foods are considered unclean and are strictly forbidden. The Qur'an [or Koran] regulates nearly every aspect of life—from the clothing one must wear to the intimacies of marriage. Those young women interviewed by Ertl are going from an American culture that has largely succumbed to the feminist agenda into a culture that severely and unapologetically restricts what women are allowed to do. Why would they voluntarily subject themselves to so many rules and restrictions?

Plato said that an excess of freedom is always followed by an excess of tyranny.[6] Doubtless the very moral breakdown that plagues contemporary Western culture contributes to the rise of Islam. People cannot live for long in a state of moral anarchy; it's little wonder they lurch to the other extreme. Women converts to Islam praise the requirement that they be "covered," saying the veils and *burqas* make them feel less like a sex object, protected from the lustful gaze of men. This is a strong indictment against the West's promiscuity. Casualties of America's broken families make Islam's rigid family values look very appealing. John Walker Lindh, remember, had to suffer through his parents' divorce, a divorce granted on the grounds that his father had taken a gay lover. No wonder he was so attracted to the legalism of the Taliban.

My own student who converted to Islam said that her new religion gave her "structure." Her life had been chaotic, but Islam gave her a rigid order to follow, one that gave her life coherence, discipline, and order. At a time when many Christian churches seek to grow by *reducing* demands on their members—minimizing doctrine and loosening up their moral teachings—Islam is growing by doing the opposite.

One of the great mysteries of the human condition—and a great proof of our twisted, sinful condition—is that legalistic religions tend to be more popular than religions of grace. People prefer the Law to the Gospel, even though the former plagues them with guilt, frustration, and moral failure. The Gospel, though, just as the Bible says—for all of its joy and liberation and life-changing grace—is offensive, a stumbling block, sheer folly (1 Corinthians 1:23).

Of course, not all legalists, nor all Muslims, go so far as to become terrorists. And yet theological issues lie at the very heart of the current conflict. If secular Western commentators cannot understand that, the other side certainly does. It is impossible to come to grips with al Qaeda and other Islamic radicals without taking their religion and the zeal it inspires seriously.

On the deepest level, Islam and Christianity are opposites. One is a religion of sheer Law. To be sure, it can be morally impressive. But it can also be intensified into a stifling, oppressive legalism, whether politically or spiritually, grounded in the fear of transgression, making it, literally, a religion of terror. The other is essentially a religion of sheer Gospel. Christianity affirms the Law, too, but always in conjunction with God's grace, which internalizes the Law and makes it an expression of freedom.

Islam and Christianity have been contending with each other for centuries. Once again, they are at war.

They are not just fighting each other, though; they are competing with each other for the soul of the twenty-first century. Western culture, which has repressed its Christian heritage until it is little more than a dim, embarrassing memory, has become so secular that it may be spiritually powerless before a militant Islam. America's very lack of religion can make it vulnerable to Islamic evangelism. Christianity, on its part, has become weak and worldly—and, forgetting its distinctiveness, has often become just as legalistic as the rest of the world's religions, with which it has become happy to identify. Only in recovering the Gospel—and the freedom it brings to those slaving under the Law—can Christianity meet the challenge of Islam.

JIHAD AND CRUSADES

Contemporary Americans tend to be oblivious to history. Since we are modern and have progressed so far, we often assume that we don't need to be aware of our history, which is long gone. But to have a culture—especially to defend a culture—requires a consciousness of history.

Certainly our adversaries do. Islamic terrorists are still mad at Western civilization because of the Crusades, even though the last one took place more than 700 years ago. When Americans hear the word *crusade,* they are probably more likely to think of Billy Graham than Richard the Lion-Hearted. But this obliviousness to medieval history does not prevent Islamic extremists from considering Americans to *be* crusaders. In the extremist mind, modern Americans are Christian crusaders deserving of being wiped out by themselves playing the role of the Saracens.

The Crusades were a sort of Christian jihad, the fruit of Christian legalism and a Christian theology of glory. The Crusades, which ravaged not just Muslims but Eastern Orthodox Christians, were a mostly shameful chapter in the history of the church. But the Crusades were only one chapter in the long war between Islam and Christianity. Muslims invaded the West long before feudal knights tried to liberate the Holy Land. In fact, there have been a number of conflicts between Muslims and the West. Perhaps significantly for our times, these often turned out to be turning points of Western civilization.

From the beginning, Islam's method of evangelism was the sword. The doctrine of *jihad*, the waging of holy war, has been toned down by the more liberal clerics to refer to internal moral struggles, but for most of the history of the religion *jihad* meant armed struggle against the enemies of Islam, conquering them and forcing them to be subject to Allah. In the century after Muhammad's death in A.D. 632, Islam conquered much of the Middle East and swept through northern Africa. Then the devout Muslim armies crossed the Strait of Gibraltar into Europe. By 715, a mere 83 years after the religion was founded, they conquered Spain. Then they crossed the Pyrenees into France with the view of conquering all of Europe for Islam.

They might have succeeded—stamping out Christianity and making the future of Europe very different from what it became—were it not for the army of Charles "The Hammer" Martel, King of the Franks, who, on October 11, 732, defeated the Moor's cavalry at Poitiers. This victory, as explained by historian Victor Davis Hanson in *Carnage and Culture: Landmark Battles in the Rise of Western Power*, not only turned back Islam. It made possible the reign of Martel's grandson, Charlemagne, who Christianized the last remaining barbarians and brought Europe out of the Dark Ages.

Later, in the time of the Reformation, the Ottoman Turks, having created one of the most extensive empires in history, invaded Europe from another direction, conquering eastern Europe, then central Europe and the Balkans. The Turks advanced on western Europe, moving into Germany and Austria.

The Turkish threat was so severe that Emperor Charles V, for all his Catholicism and his antagonism to the Reformation, did not dare attack the German nobles who were protecting Luther. He needed them to help fight the Turks. Arguably, the Turkish invasion may have allowed the Reformation to succeed. The Turks advanced as far as Vienna, where they were turned back twice, in 1529 (with the help of Lutheran soldiers) and again as late as 1683.

In between these Islamic invasions was the ill-fated invasion on the part of the Christians, the Crusades. Periodically during the Middle Ages, the Roman Catholic Church would proclaim a Crusade in an attempt to reclaim the Holy Land. Bolstered by indulgences and the conviction that if they died in the cause they would go straight to heaven, thousands of knights and peasants plundered their way to the Holy Land, sacking cities of Orthodox Christians on their way. After all, they would go to heaven no matter what they did.

The reformers condemned the Crusades as an example of the medieval trust in indulgences and works-righteousness, as if one could be saved by fighting a war instead of trusting Christ. In his answer to the papal bull condemning his teachings, Luther excoriated the Crusader mentality. "All the pope accomplishes with his crusading indulgences and his promises of heaven is to lead Christians with their lives into death and with their souls into hell," he wrote. "God does not demand crusades, indulgences, and wars. He wants us to live good lives."[7] In fact, indulgences—papal pardons for sins and remission of purgatory—were pioneered during the Crusades. They were the pope's way of recruiting and rewarding men to fight in the Holy Land. Later, indulgences were turned into a way to raise money—a scheme that one day would ignite the Reformation.

Even when the Turks invaded the West and were threatening Germany, Luther refused to sanction a religious war. Christianity is upheld by God, working through His Word and the power of the Gospel, and God does not depend on human beings to fight for Him. Christianity is a matter of the Word, Luther would say, not the sword. The emperor and the princes must indeed, in their earthly vocations, protect their people from the invaders. But even a just war must not be theologized, turned into a spiritual exercise or a meritorious service to God. "Let the Turk believe and live as he will, just as one lets the papacy and other false Christians live," wrote Luther. "The emperor's sword has nothing to do with the faith; it belongs to physical, worldly things."[8] That is to say, Christians in their earthly vocations may justly fight against those who attack them. But there can be no Christian jihad. Today's real crusaders, ironically, are the Muslim extremists who believe the very same thing as the first Crusaders—that killing infidels and dying in a jihad against their enemies will mean instant paradise.

ISLAMIC LAW

Christians think of spreading their faith in terms of evangelism, bringing the Gospel of Christ's forgiveness to individual sinners, bringing salvation to their souls for everlasting life in heaven. The Christian concern is for individual human beings. The Christian focus is transcendent. It emphasizes the spiritual reality that lies beyond this temporal, transient world, while the kingdom of heaven endures forever. Most people in the West assume that other religions work the same way: they offer a path to God, a means of salvation, a way for an individual to get to heaven.

Islam, though, has a very different preoccupation. Since it is a legalistic religion, based on the performance of good works, Muslims have no problem believing that Christians, Jews, and practitioners of other faiths might be rewarded with everlasting life in heaven. Someone who does enough good works, no matter what the religion, can earn salvation. This, no doubt, is why Islam is hailed as a "tolerant" religion.

But individual salvation is hardly the point of Islam. Muslims consider that they have spread their faith not so much when they win converts but when they have imposed Islamic law. As a Nigerian friend once said to me, when Christian missionaries come to Africa, they build schools and hospitals. When Islamic missionaries come, they try to take over the government.

For Muslims, Christianity is an insufferably otherworldly religion. Christians are so oriented to the spiritual realm that they forget their obligations here and now. They look to heaven but forget their society. Muslims look at the immorality in Western culture—the sexual permissiveness, the hedonism, the decadence—and consider Christianity a weak, impotent religion that has little moral impact.

Islam, in contrast, is this-worldly. It focuses on concrete actions and social obligations in the real world. Its laws regulate human behavior, political institutions, and nearly every detail of life in the world. It creates, or at least imposes, a culture.

The Muslim critique of Christianity stings. It is, of course, an indictment of Western culture's secularism and the decline of Christian influence. Yet Christianity *is* an otherworldly religion. It *does* look to what is eternal. It *is* skeptical of every utopia, every pretension of building heaven on earth with our own hands. This is because Christianity recognizes the scope and depth of human sin, which taints every good work apart from faith and spoils every good-sounding theory when it is applied in real life. Islam, though, insists that human society *is* perfectible, needing only the forcible application of the laws set forth in the Qur'an to create the just, utopian state here on earth. But just as individual legalists tend not to be particularly moral, remaining in a bondage to sin that they can cover up and deny but never escape, Islamic states are *not* typically just, much less utopian.

To be precise, they tend to be totalitarian. The terrorists among them—and again, not all Muslims are terrorists—have a political agenda, just as Marxist and fascist terrorists do. This was the point made by George W. Bush in his address to the joint session of Congress shortly after the September 11 attacks: "We have seen their kind before," he said of the al Qaeda terrorists. "They are the heirs of all the murderous ideologies of the twentieth century. By sacrificing human life to serve their radical visions, by abandoning every value except the will to power, they follow in the path of fascism, Nazism, and totalitarianism. And they will follow that path all the way to where it ends in history's unmarked grave of discarded lies." The terrorists are not "madmen," nor merely religious fanatics. Rather, the president was saying, they are operating out of a totalitarian political ideology.

The president, in inveighing against not just the actions of the terrorists but the content of their ideas, cited how in countries they rule, specifically Taliban-led Afghanistan, "Women are not allowed to attend school. You can be jailed for owning a television. Religion can be practiced only as their leaders dictate. A man can be jailed in Afghanistan if his beard is not long enough." Under the Taliban rule—though this holds true in most Islamic states—there is no freedom of speech or of the press, no such thing as human rights, and certainly no freedom of religion, as witness the Christian missionaries in Afghanistan who faced the death penalty for evangelism, a penalty often meted out for Muslims who convert to Christianity. To say "freedom is under attack" is not just rhetorical shorthand for describing an assault against the United States. These enemies really are against the very concept of freedom.

Christianity, in contrast, is arguably the only world religion that promises freedom. The New Testament, contrary to the common assumption that associates freedom with moral license, analyzes sin as a type of slavery. "Everyone who sins is a slave to sin," said Jesus. Sinners are in bondage, as any drug addict or drunk or sexual sinner would admit, likewise those who cannot control their temper, their appetites, or their selfish thoughts. But "if the Son sets you free, you will be free indeed" (John 8:34, 36).

Again, Christianity is the only world religion that is not all about what a person has to do. Rather, as has been said, it is all about what God does for us. That is, we are not saved by our works, but by the work of Christ, who by His grace gives us salvation as a free gift. In Christianity, virtue comes not through the imposition of external rules but from a changed heart that no longer *wants* to sin and that *wants* to love and serve others. In the connection between spiritual freedom and political freedom recognized by the American founders, someone who is virtuous from the inside does not *need* a strong political power to keep him in line. Because he governs himself, he can be, literally, self-governing. It is no accident that political freedom developed in Christian nations and nowhere else.

The Christian diagnosis—that sin is a bondage that mere Law cannot deliver us from—is borne out by abundant evidence. As those who work with international college students know, Islamic students who come to the United States often exhibit major behavioral problems. Having been brought up in a society that tries to make bad behavior impossible by Talibanlike restrictions, when they find themselves in a society without those external restraints, they often go wild. Having been physically prevented from so much as seeing a woman's skin, they cannot control themselves when they see a woman wearing today's fashions. Assuming that all American women must be making themselves sexually available since they walk around unveiled, they treat women abominably, often being accused of sexual harassment by women who are really more modest than their style of clothing might seem to indicate.

Mohamed Atta, before he commandeered the plane that rammed into the World Trade Center, prepared himself with prayer and ritual. In papers discovered after his death, he counseled his fellow soon-to-be martyrs in the piety with which they should prepare for death. And yet other evidence discovered after the attack disclosed that he and his fellow terrorists spent their last days frequenting Florida bars and strip clubs, getting drunk and paying for lapdances, despite Islam's prohibitions against alcohol, nudity, and sexual immorality. When he came to Germany to study, according to one report, he became addicted to pornography. Soon after, he began frequenting the radical Islamic mosques. Perhaps, in the sad psychology of legalism, he decided to become a martyr out of his own guilt, his moral failure before an unforgiving god impelling him to a grand gesture of self-sacrifice, doing a spectacular "good work" for the glory of Islam that would compensate for his inner shame.

In legalistic religions, morality is purely external. It must be enforced by restrictive rules or whip-bearing Virtue Police. The Law can also be softened, turned into easy-to-observe rituals. The Five Pillars of Islam are relatively easy things to *do*: repeat the testimony that "there is no God but Allah and Muhammad is His prophet," pray five times a day, give alms, fast during Ramadan, and go on a pilgrimage to Mecca during your lifetime. These actions define the life of a pious Muslim but have little moral content. The Law also can be softened by politicizing it, projecting morality away from the sinful self onto "society." Many Americans get a feeling of self-righteousness from voting the "right" way or holding to the tenets of progressive or conservative political views, despite their own deplorable personal behavior. It is possible to work for a moral society without being moral oneself.

A unique feature of Islam may be in the way it seems to allow immoral behavior in the afterlife, where it becomes a reward for being virtuous here on earth. Journalist Jack Kelley visited a Palestinian training camp that specializes in turning out suicide bombers.

He found that the young terrorists-in-training are taught that if they become martyrs—committing suicide as a human bomb or, presumably, as a pilot flying into a building—in the afterlife they will enjoy unlimited sex with 72 virgins. Kelley quotes a 16-year-old martyr-to-be in a refugee camp in Gaza, who acknowledges the political indoctrination he received but admits, "Most boys can't stop thinking about the virgins."[9] Indeed, the descriptions in Islamic writings of the sensual pleasures of the afterlife are so lurid they might be forbidden by the Taliban if they were not sacred. What is not allowed on earth is allowed in heaven. Morality is rewarded by immorality.

But even on earth, the strict rules often fall short of actual morality, accommodating the sin that lurks within. Muslims do have strong family values, but they also allow themselves to commit polygamy. Other habits sanctioned by their law—lording it over women, cruel and unusual punishments (such as cutting off the hand of a thief), persecution of Christians and other nonconformists, the jihads that can justify any atrocity—fall far short of moral perfection. Muslims, for all of their legalism and moralism, cannot escape their bondage to sin.

FREEDOM

After the Taliban retreated from Afghanistan's major cities, ordinary Afghans—though bombed and poverty-stricken—amazed Western viewers by public displays of happiness. People were playing music. (Music had been outlawed by the Taliban.) Children were flying kites. (Kite flying had also been outlawed.) People dug up television sets they had buried in their backyards and brought out photographs they had hidden, since TV and photography were also outlawed. Young men were playing soccer. (Also outlawed. One game against a Pakistani team had been allowed on the condition that the players wear long-sleeve tunics and to-the-ground trousers. The game was broken up by the Virtue Police when the Pakistani team showed up wearing shorts. Since then, the Kabul soccer field was reserved for public executions—about the only "entertainment" the Taliban allowed.)

As soon as the Taliban were routed, men lined up at barber shops to shave their beards and many women ditched the *burqa,* the wearable tent with webbed eyeholes reminiscent of the hazmat suits used in America for the anthrax scare. Both trendy styles were mandatory under the Taliban fashion police, who whipped violators with steel rods.

The smiling faces, the dancing in the streets, and the hugs for their liberators seemed surprising. Conditioned by the ideology of multiculturalism, we had assumed that the Afghans lived the austere life they did because of their *culture.* It turns out that they hated living under a regime that forbade the most innocent of pleasures. The radical Islamic regime did not reflect cultural values, just old-fashioned tyranny. Something similar is happening in Iran, no less. There is a grassroots uprising against the control-freak mullahs and their Virtue Police. The love of freedom, it appears, is multicultural.

There is political freedom, and there is cultural freedom. This must allow an individual both to voice political dissent and to act in ways that diverge from the cultural norm. Both have their origins in spiritual freedom.

No wonder Islamic rulers see Christianity as such a threat, to the point of making it a crime, punishable by imprisonment or even death, to tell someone about Jesus. If the Afghans were so happy at the merest taste of personal freedom, imagine their joy, burdened as they have been by a legalistic religion, if they could know the freedom of the Gospel.

Notes to Chapter 3

1. Patrick Sookhedo, "Anglican Priest Believes West Is Underestimating Zeal of Islam," *Washington Times,* 16 January 2002. The statistics are from the Samuel Zwemer Institute, an American missions organization.

2. Gretchen Ertl, "Converts to Islam," *National Post,* 19 January 2002.

3. Ibid. She takes the statistic from Robert Dannin, author of *Black Pilgrimage to Islam.*

4. Ertl, "Converts to Islam."

5. Ibid.

6. Plato *Republic* 564a, trans. Benjamin Jowett (Buffalo: Prometheus, 1986). This can be accessed online at plato.evansville.edu/texts/jowett/republic36.htm.

7. Martin Luther, "Defense and Explanation of All the Articles (1521)," *Luther's Works,* ed. Jaroslav Pelikan et al. (Philadelphia: Fortress Press, 1958), 32:90.

8. Luther, "On War Against the Turk," 46:184.

9. Jack Kelley, "Devotion, Desire Drive Youths to 'Martyrdom,'" *USA Today,* 9 August 2001.

4

TOLERANCE AND THE TALIBAN

America is a land of religious freedom and diversity. Unlike in other lands, people of different religions here get along. The terrorists we are fighting are very different. Their religion motivates them to hate, particularly to hate people of other religions. But these fanatics, it was thought, do not truly represent the religion they claim to follow. Conditioned by years of multicultural sensitivity training—and by the government's foreign policy concern that the coming retribution would not be interpreted as a war against Islam—Americans distinguished between the beliefs of the terrorists and actual Islam, portrayed in the media as a peaceful, tolerant religion. It is a measure of the generous-hearted spirit of Americans that, according to the polls, their respect for Islam actually shot up after September 11. It is not Islam, people were thinking, but Islamic "fundamentalists" that were to blame. The problem is not their religion but their "intolerance."

And Christians can be "fundamentalist" and "intolerant" too, which can make them just as bad.

One would think that if the hijackings, the mass murders, the tyranny of the Taliban, the gloatings of Osama bin Laden, the kidnapping and beheading of journalist Daniel Pearl, and the ongoing saga of terrorism proved anything, it would be that all religions are not the same. Not all religions are turning out suicide bombers. Some religions are apparently not benevolent. Postmodernist relativism would seem to have taken a shot from 9-11—maybe not all truth claims and moral beliefs and cultural values are equally valid after all, since some of them are capable of wreaking such carnage. Indeed, the word *evil* came back into the national vocabulary.

But, ironically, the age of terrorism has played into the hands of those who promote the unity of all religions, a theological project know as the interfaith movement. The agenda of liberal Christianity during the twentieth century was to unify the various denominations, downplaying their theological distinctions so that all of the different churches could come together in what was termed the ecumenical movement. After unifying the various Christian denominations, the next step was to unify the various *religions*, downplaying *their* religious distinctions. The ecumenical movement mutated into the interfaith movement. From this perspective, the evil of the terrorists consists in their "fundamentalism," their lack of tolerance for other religions. The answer is to affirm all faiths as valid paths to God. Expressions of religion that insist on making exclusive truth claims, privileging their own theologies above others, are to be classed with the terrorists.

Is someone who believes in the Gospel of Jesus Christ, that there is salvation under no other name (Acts 4:12), the moral equivalent of the Taliban? Again, it is easy for legalistic religions—as ultimately all non-Christian faiths are—to form interfaith agreements. After all, if the issue is being good and working your way to heaven, one path really is as good as another. Good Christians, good Muslims, good Hindus, even good atheists supposedly can earn salvation by their good works if they can come up with enough of them. But if no one has enough good works, if our sinfulness taints even the best of what we do, then everyone in the world needs a Savior. Those who cannot trust their own merit must trust Christ alone, not any of the prescriptions for good behavior or mystical ascents promised by any of the other religious systems. Legalistic Christians can join in the interfaith parade, but Gospel-believing Christians must stand apart, even in the face of cultural hostility, even when this makes them seem "irreligious."

THE ONE WORLD RELIGION

The 1,500 worshipers fill a former warehouse, now turned into a sanctuary. Before the service the congregation sings praise songs and old-time Gospel hymns, led by a 160-member choir. The service is informal and lively. Everybody hugs each other. The minister prances on the stage, preaching at full-throttle, dynamic and mesmerizing.

In the pews are celebrities, people with testimonies, many having been helped by the 31 different ministries operated by this full-service church—prison outreach, 12-step programs, support groups for troubled people, and help for the needy. Agape International Spiritual Center in suburban Los Angeles has some 7,000 members. It is a growing church, very much like the hundreds of megachurches throughout the country.

But intermixed with the Christian praise songs are the oms of Eastern meditation. In the obligatory bookstore the Bible shares space with books by gurus, self-proclaimed goddesses, and mystical pop-psychologists. The confession of faith recited by the congregation is not a creed, but "Affirmations," such as "All the power and presence of pure spirit shine forth as my experience!" and "Health and wholeness express fully as my body temple!"

Though Agape calls itself a "church," it makes no pretension of being Christian at all. Rather, as its pastor, Rev. Michael Beckwith, explains, it is "'new thought' combined with ancient wisdom." "We don't believe you are born into sin," he explained to Cathy Lynn Grossman of USA Today. "We are born into blessings. While some seek salvation, we call it 'self-elevation.'" Agape calls itself "transdenominational," but it is really transreligion. "Muslims, Jews, Christians, Buddhists, young, old, rich, poor—we cut across all lines," says Rev. Beckwith, "to reach what is true."[1]

The New Age movement has discovered the techniques of the church growth movement. Or perhaps religious entrepreneurs are realizing that Christ is the ultimate stumbling block, an obstacle to growth in this new cultural climate. The really successful churches of the emerging culture may find that they can grow most if they dispense with Christ altogether.

The project of combining the world's religions into one has been a long-standing dream for many gurus and moralists. In combining Eastern mysticism with American-style pop psychology, the New Age movement has long purported to unify the wisdom of all the world's religions. Newly invented humanistic faiths, such as Baha'i, polytheistic religions such as Hinduism, and other brands of mysticism, such as Sikhism and Zen Buddhism, have said the same thing. If religion is just a mystical experience, religious distinctions do not matter.

Roman Catholicism always seemed to be the most exclusivist creed of all. Then Vatican II opened the door for interfaith dialogue on the basis of the old Catholic error that non-Christians can be saved by following the moral light that they know. Mainline liberal Protestants, in the meantime, having emptied their own faith of its content, have even fewer hindrances in embracing other faiths. (Let leaders of other religions beware: liberal Protestants will empty other religions of their contents too.)

The aftermath of September 11 has seen scores of interfaith convocations, including a Vatican-sponsored conference at Assisi—complete with witch doctors and voodoo priests—all with their own worship space and prayer time. What do these mean? Are all of the participants in interfaith services praying to the same deity? The ecumenical activists think so. Others disagree. Some Christians feel that they need to be present to witness to the true faith in the midst of the unbelievers.

Certainly, syncretistic worship, the mingling of biblical and pagan religions, is strictly forbidden in the Bible, a violation of the First Commandment. When the Israelites brought idols of Baal into the temple, presumably because they thought that they and the Canaanites worshiped "the same god," the real God was not pleased. Some interfaith forums may not be actual worship services and may indeed—if it is allowed—be an occasion to proclaim the Gospel. But evangelism is precisely what the interfaith advocate considers anathema. To try to convert someone to a particular faith means that there is something wrong with the other person's religion. Thus, the interfaith movement, while ostensibly affirming all religions, must be hostile to the religion of the Gospel. Real Christianity is the one faith that the interfaith movement has no room for.

Christians as Taliban

The interfaith movement may be the beginning of the much anticipated "one world religion," which, though filled with moralism and religiosity, will be far different from Christianity. In his book *The Spiritual Society: What Lurks Beyond Postmodernism* Frederic W. Baue predicts the rise of a new syncretic religion, based on the premise that all of the world's religions might be combined into one.[2] Written well before September 11, the book seems eerily prophetic. Those who refuse to go along with this new interfaith religion may risk the fate of other religious nonconformists. Christians have been through this before. Rome was a multicultural, religiously diverse empire, that managed to unite its far-flung people by a system of religious tolerance based on an inclusive polytheism, which, while tolerant of faiths within its pantheon, mandated assent to the divinized state by requiring sacrifice to the emperor. Christians refused to burn the incense to Caesar, and they paid the price with their lives. But it was not just the ritual disobedience. In the anti-Christian diatribes of the time, one reason the Christians were so hated was that they professed to have the only truth.

Not that Christians are likely to face the Coliseum any time soon, but they are already hearing the same complaints. These are intensifying and growing more hostile, at least in the media and among the cultural elite, in the age of terrorism. Increasingly we are hearing that the enemy is not Islamic terrorism but intolerance. It is that intolerant, narrow-minded, restrictive view of religion that is to blame for the terrorist attacks and the Taliban oppression. Those people who think "theirs is the only true religion" are the real enemy, a charge, of course, that sticks not just to radical Muslims but to conservative Christians.

This is the way the issue is being framed by a number of commentators. Syndicated columnist Thomas Friedman writes, "World War II and the Cold War were fought to defeat secular totalitarianism." This new world war, he says, is against "religious totalitarianism." He defines religious totalitarianism as "the view that one faith must reign supreme and can be affirmed and held passionately only if all others are negated." Conservative Christians and Jews hold to this view, he says, as well as Muslims. "Can Islam, Christianity and Judaism know that God speaks Arabic on Fridays, Hebrew on Saturdays, and Latin on Sundays, and that he welcomes different human beings approaching him through their own history, out of their language and cultural heritage?" The war, says Friedman, must be fought not just on the battlefield but in houses of worship. It is urgent that the different religions "reinterpret their traditions to embrace modernity and pluralism and to create space for secularism and alternative faiths."[3] Or what? one wonders. Laser-guided precision bombs on churches that teach that Jesus is the only way for salvation?

To think so would be an overreaction. But historically when politics is mixed in with religious hostility, things can get brutal quickly. The religious dissenters can be turned into scapegoats, targets of demagogues who use their unpopularity to advance a political agenda by manipulating the public against them.

This apparently occurred to some Democrats trying to campaign against a president whose approval ratings are in the upper 80s. One strategy was to try to steal the war issue away from the Republicans by scapegoating the "religious right," presenting conservative Christians as the moral equivalent of the Taliban.

In *Newsweek's* 2001/2002 New Year's issue, forecasting what the immediate future would bring, political correspondent Howard Fineman reported,

"Democrats are planning a daring assault on the most critical turf in politics: the cultural mainstream. The theory goes like this. Our enemy in Afghanistan is religious extremism and intolerance. It's therefore more important than ever to honor the ideals of tolerance—religious, sexual, racial, reproductive—at home. The GOP is out of the mainstream, some Democrats will argue next year, because it's too dependent upon an intolerant 'religious right.'" "This is an incendiary battle plan," says Fineman, "essentially comparing the GOP right with the Taliban."[4]

Those who oppose abortion will be branded as "antiwoman," on a par with those who beat women with iron rods, deny them education, and sell them into slavery. Those whose theology motivates them to try to save innocent lives will be portrayed as being the same as those whose theology motivates them to kill innocent lives. Those who call for good music will be smeared with the same brush as those who want to abolish music altogether. A religion that has brought freedom wherever it goes will be branded as the same as a religion that has brought tyranny. Christians exercising their constitutional liberty to express their convictions in the public square will be identified with the terrorists.

Such thinking—oblivious to the actual content of beliefs—defies all logic, but contemporary thought does not particularly believe in logic. Today people tend to think in paradigms, conceptual models that shape how they think about things. In today's intellectual climate, the winner in a debate is not the person who can throw out the most facts and reasonable conclusions, but the one who can most successfully "frame the issues." The Left has successfully framed the abortion controversy as a matter of "women's rights." Euthanasia has to do with "death with dignity." Sexual immorality is framed as an issue of "freedom." Conservatives, thinking in older terms, to their credit, insist on using facts and logic to advance their arguments. But in doing so they often lose the rhetorical war, finding that their good arguments have little impact on a culture that has adopted the left-wing paradigms. This leaves the body politic particularly open to spin doctors, opinion molders, and demagogues.

Now it may be that the Christian makeup of American culture will not permit this kind of religious bigotry. Fair-minded, clear-eyed Americans might recognize such a "daring assault" on conservative Christians as real religious bigotry, the true face of religious intolerance. In fact, when Fineman's inside story was published, liberal politicians quickly denied that they would follow such a strategy. But equating cultural conservatives and the Taliban has already become the conventional wisdom in the culture-shaping worlds of academia and the arts. Christians will have to make the case that they are nothing like the Taliban and that attempts to link them—either by interfaith theologies or political propaganda—is theological terrorism.

HOSTILITY

The new hostility to orthodox Christianity goes beyond just wanting to keep moral considerations out of public policy, the preoccupation of liberal politicians. It aims also at the *theological* content of Christianity, the very substance of the faith: that salvation comes through Jesus Christ.

What galls the interfaith theologians, again, is *evangelism*. Even the private conviction that one has been saved by Christ implies that there is something wrong with all of the other ways by which people try to save themselves. If overt persecution were to ever come, it would, ironically, come in the name of religious freedom. The logic would be similar to that being used by proabortionists who are trying to cut off federal funding from Catholic and other pro-life hospitals: such institutions, they say, are denying the religious freedom of people who *believe* in abortion. Trying to get people to change their religion, through acts of evangelism and the pursuit of conversion, is violating their religious freedom to hold the religion that they already have. Already "antiproselytizing laws" are in effect in a number of countries—such as Russia, Israel, and nearly all Islamic countries.

In the same trend-spotting New Year's issue of *Newsweek* that uncovered the liberals' plan to Talibanize the Christian conservatives, religion editor Kenneth Woodward defines the kind of religious expression that the cultural elite will allow. "Mere tolerance of other religions is not enough," he says. "Even the acceptance of other religions as valid paths to God is insufficient." He says that religious people must "develop a deep understanding and appreciation of at least one other religion" in addition to their own.[5] Presumably, this means people should have at least *two* religions, in order to balance out any impermissible truth claims that any one of them might make.

By these standards the ancient Israelites should have been more inclusive in regard to idol worship; those who brought the images of Baal into the temple were exhibiting interfaith sensitivity. The early Christians should have recognized the spiritual value of Roman paganism; adding emperor worship would have made their faith more tolerant. And today, by this thinking, Christians should affirm the great teachings of Islam, the faith of their terrorist attackers.

Those who think that all religions are essentially the same can, one minute, sound generously affirming and, the next minute, attack believers in one religion for the evils of another. The Left is attacking Christians for two contradictory reasons: both for being too much like Islam and for refusing to agree with Islam.

To say that all religions are true is to say that no religion is true. The only way to bring all of them under one umbrella is to deny all of their distinctive teachings and to construct a totally new religion. This is the true disrespect for religious diversity. To not allow different beliefs, to deny the validity of any kind of distinctiveness, and to insist that everyone conform to one overarching ideology—*that* is the definition of religious totalitarianism.

If the culture is indeed drifting toward a new syncretic religion, Christians may see "new thought" churches like Agape grow bigger and bigger, as their own numbers decline. Christians will find themselves being demonized as "intolerant," perhaps our culture's worst term of abuse. Christians have endured martyrdom, but it may be even more difficult for the twenty-first century Christians to endure being unpopular.

Notes to Chapter 4

1. The description of Agape International Spiritual Center and the quotations from its minister are taken from Cathy Lynn Grossman, "Agape Gives Them 'New Thought' Religion," *USA Today*, 5 November 2001.

2. Frederic Baue, *The Spiritual Society: What Lurks Beyond Postmodernism* (Wheaton, IL: Crossway, 2001).

3. Thomas Friedman, "The Real War," *The New York Times*, 27 November 2001, p. 19.

4. Howard Fineman, "Bush's Next Challenge: Dodging No. 41's Fate," *Newsweek*, 31 December 2001/7 January 2002, p. 94.

5. Kenneth Woodward, "How Should We Think About Islam?" *Newsweek*, 31 December 2001/7 January 2002, p. 102.

5

SECULARISTS AND TERRORISM

While religious issues are a major factor in the current struggle against terrorism, secularists have much to answer for. Islam, even radical Islam, has existed for a long time without declaring all-out war against the West. It is politics when added to religion that makes such an incendiary and dangerous mixture. What precipitated the attacks of 9-11 were some distinctly Western ideas that, when grafted onto Islam, produced the terrorist mind.

The battle for Western civilization currently underway is indeed not a battle against Islam. Nor is it simply a battle against Islamic radicalism. To save the West from the enemies who would destroy it will take an intellectual battle against some of its own ideas.

THE TERRORIST WORLDVIEW

What is the mentality of someone who crashes a plane, on purpose, into a crowded building? What goes on inside the mind of someone who murders people he doesn't even know, perfect strangers who have never done him any harm?

What were they thinking? This is not just a psychological question. It also has to do with worldview. The terrorist, like everyone else, acts out of a set of assumptions about the universe, the nature of human life, and the criteria for right and wrong. The Islamic terrorists we face today are operating out of a specific worldview. Islam is part of it and culture is part of it, but those are not enough to make a terrorist, since terrorists can come out of many religions and cultures. Here are some features of a terrorist's mind-set:

Terrorists are collectivists. That is, they look at people not as individuals but in terms of the group they belong to. An Islamic radical I knew when he was a college student many years ago told me that in his view any Jew is a representative of the state of Israel. It didn't matter if that particular Jew had anything to do with Israel's policies or even if he lived in Israel. To kill a Jew, any Jew, is to strike at the whole nation of Israel. That student had no particular quarrel with America back then, but now the principle is being applied: to kill an American, any American, is to strike at America and everything it stands for.

Conversely, a collectivist will look at *himself* primarily in terms of the group he belongs to. His individuality merges with that of the group he identifies with, so that he will do *anything*—commit any crime or sacrifice his own life or even the life of his children—in the name of the community.

Terrorists think of themselves as victims. They believe their group is oppressed by some other group, which is exercising raw, arbitrary power against them. Western civilization itself is seen as nothing more than a conspiracy of oppressive power designed to keep them in their place. Nursing their injuries and their resentment, they feel perfectly justified in striking back using their own raw, arbitrary power.

Terrorists do not believe in objective morality. Right and wrong are defined solely within the closed interests of their group. By the same token, terrorists feel under no obligation to apply the values that are important within their group—such as compassion or justice—to a group they define as their enemy. There is no transcendent moral truth that applies both to them and to their enemy group. Consequently, there is no limit to the atrocities they are willing to commit against their enemy. They will do these things not only without guilt but motivated by a complete and satisfied self-righteousness.

Terrorists do not believe in objective reason. They see everything through the lens of their group grievances. Everything becomes a conspiracy against them. It is impossible to reason with them since they acknowledge no truths beyond the dogmatic ideology of their group, so that their beliefs are beyond refutation.

The belief that identity is cultural rather than individual; the conviction that Western civilization is nothing more than oppressive power of which they are victims; the rejection of transcendent, universally binding morality; the rejection of objective truth in favor of their group constructions—these ideas are being taught not only in al Qaeda terrorist-training camps, but in American universities.

For decades the academic establishment in America and Europe has been teaching this very ideology. John Sullivan, an editor of *National Review,* points out "that radical Islamism does not derive solely from Islam. It has Western as well as Islamic roots." He cites UPI commentator James C. Bennett, who has described the terrorists' ideology as the illegitimate child of "Islamic fundamentalism and neo-Marxist Western scholarship."[1]

It is no accident that the leaders of the terrorist organizations were, largely, educated at American or the even more radical European universities. They are mostly not poverty-stricken, unsophisticated refugees, nor are they usually uneducated tribesmen. While it is true that the leaders sometimes find recruits from the refugee camps to use, cynically, as suicide bombers, the terrorist networks are led and dominated by young men who are both wealthy and well educated—indeed, Western educated. The word *Taliban* means "student."

It is also no accident that the Western intellectuals who have been advocating neo-Marxism in their writings and classrooms are criticizing America's war effort and are playing the role of apologist for the terrorists. For the last several decades, professors have been waging a secular jihad against Western civilization, not just eliminating academic requirements (as Jesse Jackson chanted at Stanford, "Hey, ho, hey, ho, Western Civ has got to go"), but deconstructing its greatest accomplishments (dismissing Shakespeare, the Constitution, Christianity, and the like for being racist, sexist, and oppressive). This has spilled over into the public schools and the popular culture, but it resonates most powerfully in the Third World, where students trying to learn from the West also have engraved into their minds just how oppressed they are by the postcolonial power structures that continue to control the world.

Certainly the European legacy of colonialism—in which England and France ruled much of the Muslim world—is a shameful one, and the dismantling of colonialism in the twentieth century left behind problems of its own. And the founding of the state of Israel by Western powers infuriated the Muslim world in ways that are impossible to overstate. Added to this is the humiliation the Islamic world feels—from the many Israeli victories over Arab armies to the vast prosperity and technological achievement of the West, in such contrast to the weakness of their supposedly God-ordained Islamic cultures. All of this contributes to Islamic rage.

But the form it takes, its ideology, is shaped by postmodernist political thought, which analyzes *all* social issues in terms of oppression, power, and exploitation. Whereas the Marxists interpreted culture in terms of a class struggle between the middle class and the workers, "post-Marxists," or "neo-Marxists," focus on the power struggle between other kinds of groups—feminists reduce the complexities of culture, politics, art, and religion to the dynamic of men oppressing women; the so-called "queer theorists" do the same with heterosexuals oppressing gays; racial scholars reduce everything to the white race exploiting "people of color." The rhetoric of Islamic radicals is shaped by postcolonialist thought, which interprets the world in terms of the conflict between the rich nations of the West and the "developing nations" of the Third World. Borrowing heavily from old-fashioned Marxism in its preoccupation with economics and in its condemnation of the West as "imperialist" and "colonialist," this kind of analysis is "neo-Marxist" also in its call for revolution.

All of these brands of postmodernism cultivate a sense of collectivism, victimhood, moral relativism, and subjective truth.

ISLAMIC FASCISM

Postmodernism would seem to accord with Islam no better than it does with Christianity. And, indeed, the Muslim brand of neo-Marxism took a distinctly Islamic turn. Islamic radicals have no sympathy with feminism or gay rights. Islam certainly teaches moral absolutes. And yet, at the same time, morality does become relative in the terrorist mind when it comes to killing innocent men, women, and children in symbolic gestures for their cause.

Liberal Islamic scholars are adamant that such actions cannot be sanctioned by Islam. According to Islamic law, they point out, suicide is an unforgivable sin and terrorism is punishable by death. "Classical Islamic law explicitly prohibits the taking or slaying of hostages," observed Islamic scholar Khaled Abou El

Fadl. "Furthermore, it prohibits stealth or indiscriminate attacks against enemies, Muslim or non-Muslim."

What we have instead with the Islamic terrorists, says El Fadl, is something new: "This brand of Islamic theology is largely dismissive of the classical juristic tradition and of any notion of universal and innate moral values."[2]

The great cultural contribution of monotheism— Jewish, Christian, Muslim—was the notion of transcendence, that God and the moral truths He reveals and embodies transcend nature, the individual, and the culture itself. Nature is not divine, so it can be studied. Leaders are not divine, so they can be criticized. Society is not divine, so it can be changed. This notion of a transcendent spiritual reality over and above the material order opened the door for science, rationality, human rights, and social progress.

In the West these notions came under attack by a group of thinkers and social activists that became known as fascists. In his classic study of the movement, *The Three Faces of Fascism*, Ernst Nolte summarizes the ideology as "the practical and violent resistance to transcendence."[3]

Fascists sought to channel people's religious energy into the here and now, away from a transcendent God, onto a divinized state. Many of them sought to re-create the old pagan ideal, in which nature, the community, and the leader were all one continuum with the gods. They rejected individualism in favor of group identity. They minimized reason in favor of emotion and cultivated a primitive mysticism devoted to blood and the soil. They rejected universal moral values in favor of instinct, emotional release, and the will to power.

They also had an economic theory: national socialism. Hailed as a third way between capitalism and communism, the fascist brand of socialism allowed for some private property but mandated that it be controlled by the state and used for the good of the nation.

This is essentially what the terrorists and the states that support them believe. For them, Islam is not so much a transcendent faith as an immanent sacred society. There are no universal moral values; instead, whatever the sacred political program does is morally right—including such things as suicide, mass murder, and crashing airplanes into skyscrapers.

The Middle Eastern terrorists also have an economic ideology, which is nothing less than national socialism. This is particularly true in the countries that support the terrorists. Perhaps the best manifesto of contemporary fascism is the *Green Book* by Libya's Muammar al-Gadhafi. In it, this self-proclaimed "Leader of the World Revolution" develops the "Third Universal Theory," his alternative to both capitalism and communism. Al-Gadhafi identifies "nature" with "religion," offers a political order based on the unity of the people in their national identity, and describes a socialism that allows people to own their houses and cars but eliminates the private ownership of land and resources. Point by point, the *Green Book* (all of which is posted online) echoes what Mussolini was writing in the last century.

So does the Arab Socialist Ba'th Party of Iraqi President Saddam Hussein. Its ideology is described in a propaganda Web site as being "characterized by a leadership of a revolutionary party which possesses a national ideology of power."

Neither al-Gadhafi's *Green Book* nor Hussein's Ba'th party have much to say about Islam. Both were originally presented as wholly secular ideologies. Only recently—since the Gulf War—have the two wrapped themselves in the rhetorical robes of Islam. At first their intention was to create a secular state. Nevertheless, they have found that tapping into an uninformed religious zeal can give them a sacred status among their followers, whom they can then motivate to do whatever they are told in the name of their faith. Conversely, conservative Muslims, inspired by elements within Islam itself—such as the project of establishing a sacred state under Islamic law—could ally themselves with this brand of politics and its tactics.

Another characteristic of fascism of every stripe is the hatred of the Jews. This is more than resentment of Jewish capitalists or Israeli settlements in Palestine, though such resentments are useful in drumming up popular support. For the fascists, the "Jewish influence" is precisely that transcendence—of God, of universal moral truths, of the kinds of thought and political freedom this implies—that they hope to do away with. One difference is that the fascism of the Middle East recognizes what the Western fascists believed in private but drew back from saying in public, that if the Jews are the enemy, so are Christians.

As I have shown in my book *Modern Fascism,* there is a connection between fascism and postmodernism. They share common ancestors (Nietzsche, Heidegger) and common doctrines (collectivism, relativism, subjectivism, cultural determinism).[4] Now, throw in Islam, and the mixture is explosive.

POSTMODERNISM AFTER 9-11

For Americans, September 11 when the planes crashed was a cultural turning point. Suddenly all of the relativism, the pop-culture shallowness, and the cynical posing of postmodernism seemed irrelevant. Suddenly Americans awakened to the realization that their civilization, after decades of unanswered assaults, is worth defending.

Postmodernists rejected the very possibility of objective truth, insisting that reality is nothing more than a construction of the culture or of the mind. The planes that came out of nowhere to crash into buildings and into every American's consciousness were no mental constructions. Objective reality, with all of its hard edges, reasserted itself.

Postmodernists rejected the very possibility of objective morality. What is right or wrong varies, they said, according to the culture or the individual. If a person *chooses* certain values, that makes them right for that person. The terrorists certainly made a *choice,* and what they did was right *for them.* But somehow their cold-blooded murder of thousands of ordinary men, women, and children was seen as pure, objective evil, something postmodernists had professed not to believe in.

Postmodernists believed that all cultures are equally valid, that we have no basis for saying that one kind of society or way of thinking is better than any other. Actually, one culture is worse than all the rest according to the postmodernist curriculum, namely, Western civilization. When that civilization was attacked, though, it began to be seen as something worth defending. It became hard to consider the havens of Islamic terrorism, which teach hatred, oppression, and suicide bombing, as really being equal to the land of the free.

New York City is, arguably, the capital of America's culture—the home of the publishing industry, the playground of the intellectual elite, the great media center, the epicenter of the art world, and the home of the trendsetters and the fashion industry. Suddenly their sensibility changed.

A characteristic trait of the postmodernist attitude is irony. Since nothing is real and everything is fake, nothing can be taken seriously. Everything becomes a joke, and the cool persona is someone who goes through life with a sense of detached, cynical irony. Yet after the attack Jerry Seinfeld, the personification of New York cynical comedy, was putting together a benefit for the victims. David Letterman, the king of mockery, was comforting Dan Rather on *Late Show with David Letterman,* both of them close to tears.

Hip publications like the online magazine *Salon* were printing testimonials from self-confessed flag-burners turned flag-wavers. Intellectuals, novelists, and artists were changing their tunes like musicians in Carnegie Hall. What had once been fashionable in the avant garde world of the arts now was now seen to be in embarrassingly bad taste.

The New York art scene, for example, was dominated by artists' attempt to shock. Art that attacked America was no longer so attractive now that America was under attack. The purposeful creation of ugliness no longer seemed as clever in light of the real ugliness that hung in the air of New York. Some artists had been doing things like carving up human corpses and displaying photographs of the results—in light of the body parts in the rubble of the World Trade Center, this no longer seemed amusing. One artist, playing the old part, proclaimed that the collapse of the World Trade Center towers was the greatest work of art of all time. According to the aesthetics of shock and the standards of violent performance art, it probably was. But the New York art world, grieving like the rest of the city, was unimpressed with the bon mot, condemning his statement for its tastelessness and gross insensitivity—sort of like what ordinary Americans had been saying about some of the creations of the New York art world. The artist who hailed the World Trade Center collapse had his retrospective cancelled and found himself ostracized by his peers.

It had become fashionable among the cultural elite to ridicule the ordinary people who could never understand the esoteric experimentation of the art world or the sophisticated subtleties of the intellectualoids. But now everyone was hailing the "heroism" of the blue collar cops and firefighters who died trying to rescue the office workers and who continued to wear themselves out combing through the rubble.

Voices in the art world began calling for a new movement, one that is more "human" than the slick cynicism that had ruled before. The *New York Times* asked artists what the attack will now mean for the arts. Pulitzer-prize winning composer John Corigliano called for the recovery of "our titanic richness of musical resource with unmistakable structural order." Songwriter Paul Simon, of Simon and Garfunkel fame, noted the sounds of silence after the attack, the "almost total absence of the popular culture from the nation's airwaves." He went on to condemn the nihilism that has dominated the arts and predicted a big change. "We should recognize that seismic events impact on the creative process and that artistic and spiritual rebirth can follow a shattering experience."[5]

True, left-wing academics like Noam Chomsky and Susan Sonntag kept up their old lines. Agreeing with Osama bin Laden, they insisted that the terrorist attacks were justified because of America's imperialism, its support of Israel, and oppression of the developing world. But the post-Marxists on university campuses were making fools of themselves, to the point that it was evident even to most college students.

As Andrew Sullivan, editor of the liberal *New Republic,* pointed out, the leftists were putting themselves in the uncomfortable position of supporting an ideology that brutally subjugates women (to the point of flogging them for walking by themselves in public), executes homosexuals, and outlaws every human free-dom. People who have made their careers by condemn-ing America for being antiwoman, homophobic, and oppressive were now defending a regime that really *is* all of these things. And anyone who compares New York City to Afghanistan has to admit that America is a free country, after all, that it has ideals worth defending.[6]

MILITANT SECULARISM

So what will contemporary American culture turn to next? Perhaps it will go back to the broader, richer worldviews that preceded both the narrow ratio-nalism of the modernists and the still-narrower rela-tivism of the postmodernists. Maybe classicism, Amer-ican republicanism, or even Christianity might come back into vogue. Or maybe the reversion will go back even further, to paganism, a new world religion that is only a contemporary form of a primitive, destructive spirituality. There are signs of all of these, all of which may flourish, at least for awhile, at the same time.

Another option, though, may be a reaction against all religion, the rise of a new militant secular-ism. The fundamentalisms of both Islam and Chris-tianity are the enemy of freedom and pleasure that can only be known by embracing sheer material existence, without moral rules or theological limitations.

This seems to be the stance promoted by novelist Salman Rushdie. To be sure, he has the credentials to oppose terrorism. He was the writer who was sen-tenced to death by a Muslim *fatwa,* a decree from an Islamic council condemning the novelist, who was

born a Muslim, for disrespecting the prophet Muhammad in his novel *The Satanic Verses.* Having had to live
in hiding for decades, Rushdie finally emerged cau-
tiously back into the public and moved to New York
City—just in time to watch the towers fall and to find
his adopted city experiencing its own *fatwa.* In a col-
umn for the *Washington Post,* Rushdie takes to task the
anti-American Left. He then urges the exaltation of
everything that "fundamentalists" of every stripe are
against:

> The fundamentalist believes that we believe in
> nothing. In his world-view, he has his absolute
> certainties, while we are sunk in sybaritic indul-
> gence. To prove him wrong, we must first know
> that he is wrong. We must agree on what matters:
> kissing in public places, bacon sandwiches, dis-
> agreement, cutting-edge fashion, literature, gen-
> erosity, water, a more equitable distribution of
> the world's resources, movies, music, freedom of
> thought, beauty, love. These will be our weapons.
> Not by making war but by the unafraid way we
> choose to live shall we defeat them. The funda-
> mentalist seeks to bring down a great deal more
> than buildings. Such people are against, to offer
> just a brief list, freedom of speech, a multi-party
> political system, universal adult suffrage,
> accountable government, Jews, homosexuals,
> women's rights, pluralism, secularism, short
> skirts, dancing, beardlessness, evolution theory,
> sex. It is easy to be against terrorism. But what
> are we for? What will we risk our lives to defend?
> Can we unanimously concur that all the items in
> the above list—yes, even the short skirts and
> dancing—are worth dying for?[7]

Just as the Romans were unwilling to die for their orgies in the face of the barbarian onslaught, Americans, though open to many things on that list, are probably unwilling to die for such things as evolution, homosexuality, and short skirts. Nevertheless, like the interfaith theologians, militant secularists lump together conservative Christians with the Muslim terrorists as "fundamentalists," as the enemy who deserves to be eradicated. Again, Christians must prove them wrong. This must entail highlighting the distinctiveness of the Christian Gospel, which bears fruit in both freedom and morality, as opposed to the barren social theories and sin-producing legalism not only of Islam, but of Western secularism.

Notes to Chapter 5

1. John Sullivan, "Mosque Mission: Dealing with Radical Islamism," *National Review Online*, 9 October 2001.

2. Khaled Abou El Fadl, "What Became of Tolerance in Islam?" *Los Angeles Times*, 14 September 2001.

3. Ernst Nolte, *The Three Faces of Fascism* (New York: Holt, Rinehart & Winston, 1965), p. 429.

4. See Gene Edward Veith, *Modern Fascism: Liquidating the Judeo-Christian Worldview* (St. Louis: Concordia Publishing House, 1993).

5. Paul Simon, John Corigliano et al., "Music: The Aftermath," *The New York Times*, 23 September 2001.

6. Andrew Sullivan, "The Agony of the Left," *Wall Street Journal*, 10 October 2001.

7. Salman Rushdie, "Fighting the Forces of Invisibility," *The Washington Post*, 2 October 2001, p. A25.

6

CHRISTIAN CITIZENSHIP

One of the overriding feelings that swept over Americans on September 11, as everyone watched the replay of the airliner crashing into the building over and over again, was a sense of unity, that we as Americans were all in this together. Our empathy for those who lost their lives in the towers and the Pentagon and our pride in our fellow citizens who stormed the hijackers over Pennsylvania created a shared national identity that we were not used to. Southerners, small town Midwesterners, and farmers in the West felt their hearts go out to New York City. New York City!

The sense of patriotism was palpable. The flags came out—on the lapels of previously cynical journalists, on car antennas. There was the flag-raising at ground zero, in a photograph whose very angles were reminiscent of the flag-raising at Iwo Jima. And that tattered flag dug out of the rubble of the World Trade

Center flew at the World Center and at the Winter Olympics! Hardly any American—conservative or liberal, black or white, working man or wealthy sophisticate—stood apart from the spirit of national unity. After all, those who died were killed for one reason only. They were Americans. (Yes, people from many other nations died, too, but the target was America and Americans.) Moreover, those who were killed were just like us. They were Americans from all walks of life, the whole range of races and social classes and income levels, just going to work or going about their day-to-day business. It could have happened to any of us. We felt a bond with those who died. We were fellow Americans.

We were not used to this national unity, this sense of common citizenship and the ties that it means. We were still in the shadow of a bitterly divisive, even disputed election. And yet now the distinction between the "red state" folks and the "blue state" folks, whose values were considered so different and incompatible, vanished. Many Americans who had become used to criticizing the president and scorning their government now rallied behind their national leaders. Many Baby Boomers, their political values shaped by protests against the Vietnam War, felt a desire for military action they had never known before. Just as there had always been an anti-Americanism on the Left, there had arisen an anti-Americanism on the Right, with many conservatives—frustrated by liberal policies, an overly intrusive central government, and an increasingly permissive and decadent society—hating their culture and, in some cases, questioning the very legitimacy of their government. Now Americans set aside their differences and rallied around the flag.

Christians in particular had become somewhat ambiguous about their country. It had seemed to abandon its Christian heritage, becoming just another secular Leviathan. That the United States had legalized abortion, resulting in a holocaust of monumental proportions, made it lose its moral legitimacy. When Christians tried to be active politically, they were mostly first used and then abandoned, once the candidates they supported got into office.

But now, when the president called for prayers, churches and individual believers gladly obliged. The church seemed relevant to the state once again. And the state seemed relevant to the church. Indeed, Christians once again felt the old stirrings of citizenship.

CHURCH AND STATE

Christians have always struggled with the best way to relate their faith to their citizenship. For Islam, of course, there is no problem. There is to be no difference between the faith and the social order, with Islamic law governing both individuals and the state. That Christians have tended to feel a tension between their spiritual lives and their lives in the world demonstrates a profound difference with other religions. Most religions are cultural religions, existing to give divine sanction to an earthly culture. Not only Islam but Hinduism and the various tribal pagan religions function in this way. To become a Hindu or a Muslim is to adopt a culture.

Christianity, by contrast, is for all cultures, for people "from every nation, tribe, people and language" (Revelation 7:9). When Christianity gets indistinguishable from the culture—as it did in the Holy Roman Empire and the state churches of Europe—it loses its spiritual edge and falls into the complacent materialism of the sin known as "worldliness." And yet the Bible is clear that secular government does have a God-ordained authority. In his classical theological treatise *Christ and Culture,* Richard Niebuhr describes the various possible relationships between the two, each of which has had its adherents in the history and the different theologies of Christianity.[1]

One possibility is to put culture above Christ, that is, to have the secular society establish the values, beliefs, and practices of the church. As the National Council of Churches (NCC) puts it, the world sets the agenda for the church. If the culture changes, Christianity must change accordingly. This is the path of *liberal theology.*

There are, of course, many varieties of liberal theology, since cultures vary over time and space. From the mainline denominations represented by the NCC to evangelicals who think the church has to reinvent itself to become culturally relevant, they are all treating the culture as authoritative. Demands that churches change their understanding about what the Bible teaches about women's ordination to accommodate the feminists, that they loosen up their teachings about sexual morality in light of changing values, that they revise their teachings about the Godhead and the deity of Christ to fit the latest academic philosophy, and that they throw out their theologies of worship to follow the styles of the pop culture are all manifestations of a *liberal* theology.

Among the problems of this approach is that it turns Christianity into a cultural religion. Social trends and fashions replace the Word of God as the church's authority, and the church even loses its ability to criticize the culture. The church withers away since it is really no longer needed. It loses the transcendence of its message and, invariably, stops proclaiming the Gospel. Though liberal theology is often accompanied by liberal politics, it need not be, as the liberal churches of Germany during the Hitler regime demonstrate. Under this approach, the state is divinized, just as it is under Islam.

Another of Niebuhr's options is to place Christ above culture, to have the church rule the state.[2] Christianity offers the way to a just society, correcting its evils and governing every facet of life. This has been the way of medieval popes and Puritan commonwealths, of nineteenth-century social reformers, twentieth-century liberation theologians, and Christian political activists of both the Left and the Right.

What this does, though, is to make Christianity a religion of *Law* and give the church a this-worldly focus at the expense of its true mission to proclaim the Gospel and to bring people to eternal life in heaven. The fact is, no one and no culture can keep God's Law. No one can be forced into Christianity, since personal faith is a gift of God and cannot be coerced. When the church, historically, has assumed earthly power, the result has been corruption in both church and culture. The church by definition becomes worldly, and the culture is made sacred. The result is a divinized state, along with a secularized church. Christianity is reduced to a cultural religion. In its concern for acquiring power and for building the kingdom of heaven on earth through human works, this position is a theology of glory, a religion of works rather than the grace of God. This is the position that most closely resembles that of Islam. Though the current secularist charges are a slander, there could indeed arise a Christian Taliban.

Another possibility cited by Niebuhr is Christ against culture. This view recognizes the innate sinfulness of all human institutions and calls Christians to separate from the corrupt culture, withdrawing into distinct Christian communities. The church becomes an *alternative* to the mainline culture, with Christians refusing to take part in the culture of the world.

This has been the approach of the early monastic movement, the anabaptist subcultures, fundamentalist separatism, and the various experiments in Christian communal living. The Amish are a good example of a group of Christians who refuse to compromise with the worldly culture, rejecting military service, contemporary dress, and modern technology as being unworthy of their commitment to radical discipleship.

And yet Jesus explicitly said in His prayer at Gethsemane, "My prayer is not that You take them out of the world. . . . As You sent Me into the world, I have sent them into the world" (John 17:15–18). The option of separatism, in forming a Christian subculture, has the effect of reducing Christianity to a cultural religion. The "church," far from being a universal, transcultural institution, becomes just another culture. Thus, the Amish end up defining themselves by their beards and buggies rather than by a universal Gospel. Separatist churches define themselves in terms of what its members must *do* rather than what God has done for them. The Law has a way of driving out the Gospel, leaving a religion based on works instead of grace. They also neglect the way God does rule throughout His creation, including the social orders, even among those who do not know Him. Separatism, in setting a divinized culture over and against a demonic culture, approximates the way Islamic radicals see themselves in a godless world against which they must wage war.

The possibility for the relationship between Christ and culture that seems to best account for what Scripture says is what Niebuhr calls "Christ and culture in paradox." Luther calls it the doctrine of the two kingdoms. This view accounts for the insights of the other positions, acknowledging that we are cultural creatures, that God is sovereign over every sphere of life, that we live in a sinful and fallen world, and that Christians must both be separate from the world and actively involved in it. And it avoids the danger that Christians might take upon themselves the role of the Taliban.

According to this view, God is the king of both the church and the culture, but He rules the two in different ways. In the church God reigns through the work of Christ and the giving of the Holy Spirit, who is active in His Word and Sacraments, both of which express His love and grace by bestowing the forgiveness of sins and calling sinners into the life of faith. In the world God also exercises His authority and His control over all of creation. He upholds the very universe, so that the laws of physics, the processes of chemistry, and other natural laws are part of what He has ordained. Similarly, God rules the nations—even those who do not acknowledge Him—making human beings to be social creatures in need of governments, laws, and cultures to mitigate the self-destructive tendencies of sin and to care for the welfare of all of His creatures.

Thus, God has a spiritual rule in the hearts and lives of Christians; He also has a secular rule that extends throughout His creation and in every culture. God reigns in the church through the Gospel, the proclamation of forgiveness in the cross of Jesus Christ, a message that kindles faith and an inward transformation in the believer. He reigns in the world through His Law, which calls human societies to justice and righteousness, and through vocation, in which He works through human beings to whom He has given special callings for service to their neighbors.

A Christian is thus a citizen of two kingdoms— the kingdom of heaven and the kingdom of this world. These spheres have different demands and operate in different ways. But God is the king of both. Because the secular sphere, in its culture and government, is in itself part of God's domain, in its very secular functioning, Christians are to be engaged *in* the world.

They are not *of* the world, however, since this world
will pass away, while Christians will enjoy their citizenship in heaven forever. The secular kingdom—though
in a state of constant conflict with sin and the devil—
is a fitting arena for Christian action, though it
includes nonbelievers, as well, who also have their
offices through which God works.

MORALITY

That God rules, in a hidden way, even among
those who do not know Him, means that the so-called
"kingdom of the left hand," His secular domain, opens
up a vast upon that Christians do share with non-
Christians.

Take morality, for instance. According to this
view, morality is *not* merely a matter of religion. Efforts
are made to silence those who oppose abortion on the
grounds that they are "trying to impose their religion
on everybody else." But morality is not the same as religion. A Christian does not have some unique brand of
morality; rather, what makes a Christian is the Gospel.
Morality is for everyone. Protecting innocent life
should be a foundational principle for all societies, of
whatever religion or culture.

The doctrine of the two kingdoms insists that
God's Law is transcendent in its scope and its authority.
As C. S. Lewis has shown in *The Abolition of Man*, it is
simply not true that every culture and every religion
has its own morality. Principles of justice, honesty,
courage, and responsibility to one's neighbor are universal.[3] Though revealed most fully in Scripture, God's

Law is written on the hearts even of the unbelieving Gentiles (Romans 2:14–16).

It is not our *morality* that defines Christians. This we share with other religions and many secularists. What defines Christians is our *faith*. We do not claim to have a superior moral code; rather, we claim to have found a solution to the fact that we and the rest of the world have not lived according to the moral code that we already have. We teach *forgiveness*. We teach God's *grace*. "We preach Christ crucified" (1 Corinthians 1:23).

This is the distinct message of Christianity: the Gospel, not the Law, which we share with others. That Christians can be so easily confused with the Taliban is perhaps a testimony to the fact that Christians have often obscured their message—perhaps forgetting this themselves and slipping into legalism—failing to convey before the rest of the world that their faith is one of grace and forgiveness.

To be sure, Christians believe in God's moral Law. A strenuous, uncompromising understanding of moral truth is necessary; otherwise, no one would grasp his desperate need for a Savior. And in today's cultural climate, morality itself is under attack. Certainly, Christians must be in the fray defending it. In this they can join with others who do not share their faith. Today's moral relativism is no theoretical issue, but it manifests itself in horrible evil. If terrorism has to do with the mass murder of innocent people, then abortion is terrorism on a scale that dwarfs 9-11.

The reformers distinguished between three uses of the Law. God's secular domain is under His moral

Law, what the reformers called "the first use of the Law." Sometimes called "the civil use," the Law in this sense restrains evil, promoting outward conformity to what is right, so that sinful human beings can live in at least a rough harmony with each other. Otherwise, the power of sin would be such that no human society would be possible—all would be rape, carnage, and anarchy. Families, cultures, and governments enforce certain standards of behavior. Obeying the civil use of the Law saves no one, of course, since the sin that lurks inside still condemns us. No one can claim a right to heaven because he was a good, law-abiding citizen, but such virtues do indeed have great value. When someone knows himself as a sinner, though, acknowledging his guilt and moral failure, he is feeling the Law's second use, "the theological use of the Law," a prelude to the Gospel. Then and only then can he live out the "third use of the Law," motivated from within by the Gospel to live in a way that pleases God.

Christians dare not confuse the Gospel with the Law. Christianity, unlike every other world religion, is *not* all about what we must *do*. It is about what Christ has done for us. There can be no question for Christians of setting up either a theocratic regime or a secularist utopia. We have too realistic a view of sin to imagine that any such theoretical scheme, however good it might sound on paper, would actually work in a fallen world. Christianity is utterly realistic in recognizing human and social and governmental limits. This is a major difference with Islam. It may be, as Muslims say, that the Qur'an offers principles for a benevolent and just society, that if only Islamic law were applied consistently, everyone would live happily ever after. This is the ideal. But with the implacable fact of sin that cannot be eradicated by external rules, here is the reality: obliteration of music, games, art, and other innocent pleasures, plus brutal oppression, executions in soccer fields, and women getting whipped with steel rods.

Christians *could not* set up a society like that, though this is the impression created by the critics who want to silence us. Though some may have tried, and though some Christians create a Talibanlike impression, the actual legacy of the Christian influence on nations and on governments has been political and individual and religious freedom.[4]

THE TWO KINGDOMS AND AMERICA

The doctrine of the two kingdoms, while articulated by Luther, is not just a peculiarly Lutheran dogma. It is the way most Christians actually live out their lives in the world. It was certainly influential in the American constitutional principle of the separation of church and state, which was not the Jeffersonian "wall," as is often assumed, but a distinction between two mutually supporting spheres, which has, historically, caused both to thrive. The state may not coerce an individual's inner life and convictions and may not try to establish some "cultural religion" to give itself a transcendent authority. A church, though, has its own sphere, which is protected from governmental interference. Believers may not be persecuted or silenced by the state.

God, though, was understood as the king of both church and state. His authority over the nation was not expressed in a churchly, nor even distinctly religious manner, but He was recognized as the ground of all morality and the basis for the value and dignity of human life. As expressed in America's founding document (emphasis added), "We hold these truths to be self evident, that all men *were created* equal, and that they *were endowed by their Creator* with certain inalienable rights." God was also recognized as the power that rules and governs human events, controlling all of history by His will. Thus, the founders of America committed their cause to "almighty providence." The founders began their deliberations with prayer, supported chaplains in the legislature and the armed forces, and—in a pattern repeated by presidents from Washington, through Lincoln, to George W. Bush—would ask churches to join in special days of prayer for the nation.

The founders went further in maintaining that a free society could *only* succeed if the people were religious. They reasoned this way: people do have sinful impulses, which not only revelation but practical experience daily confirms. Those inclined to steal, destroy, and commit mayhem against their neighbors have to be restrained by the power of the state. The more overt evil that is committed, the more police officers will be needed, just to maintain the public safety. Conversely, if people control *themselves,* they will not need so much external control from an overly powerful government. If their moral sensibility comes from the *inside,* from a spiritual transformation that makes them want to do what is right of their own free will, then there will be no need for a coercive and potentially tyrannical government. Even a democracy could become coercive and tyrannical if the people were too easily swayed by their passions and vices. People who can govern themselves, quite literally, can become self-governing.

Corollaries of the doctrine of the two kingdoms abound in the theory and practice of political freedom. The government itself is limited, since it, too, is under the higher authority of God and is subject to criticism and reform according to His higher moral Law. Since faith cannot be coerced, the individual conscience is to be free. Religion is not to be restricted by the state. Preachers or theologians may not be silenced or their expression controlled. Such theological principles loom behind the origin of the freedom of speech and the freedom of the press.[5] Christian realism about how sin can infect the noblest of institutions lies behind the "checks and balances" built into the constitutional separation of powers, whereby each branch of government is prevented from overreaching.

It must be remembered, though, that not just Americans and not just nations of Christians but all human societies are governed by God, working in a hidden way. This is true of Muslim nations, too, as God works through their families and leaders and legal systems to restrain evil. Both America and Muslim nations must worry about the way sin distorts policies and state practices. Illegitimate rulers, those who have usurped power against the laws of their own states, are also a problem throughout the world. No one elected the Taliban, who overthrew the legitimate government of Afghanistan, and therefore, like Saddam Hussein and Kim Jong Il, ruled as dictators rather than as lawful authorities.

Still, the doctrine of the two kingdoms affirms the legitimacy of cultures and governments, in all of their diversity. This is the true basis for a legitimate "multiculturalism," one that sees God Himself as being present and active in human institutions, even where He is not known. But it avoids the trap of cultural and moral relativism, since God's moral Law—and the principles of justice and human rights that it encodes—judges all cultures and pushes them all to moral reformation.

CITIZENSHIP AS VOCATION

The doctrine of the two kingdoms teaches that God governs human societies not only by means of the moral Law but also by means of vocation. This means that citizenship in their societies is not just an option for Christians. It is a divine calling.

According to the doctrine of vocation, Christians—in addition to their callings in the family, the church, and the workplace—have a calling to be citizens. God works through earthly rulers; He puts us Christians under their authority, and He calls us into the responsibilities of good citizenship.

We have already looked at Romans 13, which spells out how God is hidden in secular government. "Everyone must submit himself to the governing authorities, for there is no authority except that which

God has established. The authorities that exist have been established by God" (13:1).

Since God is the only one who can claim absolute authority in Himself, lesser offices derive their authority from His. The text also speaks about the purpose of earthly governments: to punish wrongdoers, to "bear the sword." Moreover, the earthly governor is God's servant, God's "agent." In other words, just like God gives daily bread through the means of the farmer, He deals out punishment to evildoers and protects law-abiding citizens through the means of the governing authorities.

Romans 13 makes many Christians squirm, especially when they live under bad rulers. Are we *always* supposed to submit to our rulers? Even the Hitlers of the world? Should the Christian missionaries imprisoned by the Taliban obey the law in Afghanistan not to proclaim the Gospel?

The Augsburg Confession, article XVI, says that "Christians owe obedience to their magistrates and laws except when commanded to sin. For then they owe greater obedience to God than to human beings."[6] The confessors cite Acts 5:29, when the disciples were forbidden by law to preach the Gospel: "We must obey God rather than men."

But there is a special twist for Americans and others who live under a democratic republic, that is to say, those who have been called to be citizens in such a system. Who is the "governing authority"? While we do have magistrates and legal authorities to whom we are subject, how are they put into office and to whom do they answer? In this kind of government, which lacks kings and emperors, rulers are themselves subject to the people. We elect our governing officials. Ultimately, *we* rule *them*.

This means that the calling of citizenship in a free society entails responsibilities of rule as well as submission. Citizens must be engaged in the workings of their government. This entails not only voting but voting in a reflective way, taking responsibility for the policies that are at stake, keeping track of the performance of the elected representatives, and removing from office those who need to be in a different vocation. To perform this high office, citizens must keep up with events and policy debates and formulate their own opinions about the policies their government should follow.

Scripture says quite a bit about Christians' obligation to perform the duties of citizenship, such as paying their taxes (Matthew 22:15–21; Romans 13:6–7). The Christian's civic duties are summarized by St. Peter:

> Submit yourselves for the Lord's sake to every authority instituted among men: whether to the king, as the supreme authority, or to governors, who are sent by Him to punish those who do wrong and to commend those who do right. For it is God's will that by doing good you should silence the ignorant talk of foolish men. Live as free men, but do not use your freedom as a cover-up for evil; live as servants of God. Show proper respect to everyone: Love the brother-

hood of believers, fear God, honor the king.
(1 Peter 2:13–17)

This is a formula not for slavish passivity but for freedom. "Live as free men."

The Christian's civic duty includes prayer: "I urge, then, first of all, that requests, prayers, intercession and thanksgiving be made for everyone—for kings and all those in authority, that we may live peaceful and quiet lives in all godliness and holiness. This is good, and pleases God our Savior, who wants all men to be saved and to come to a knowledge of the truth" (1 Timothy 2:1–4). This text supports the doctrine of the two kingdoms, teaching that God's care extends to "all people" and to "all who are in high positions." It also pictures Christians not as subversive rebels, as their enemies claimed and as some of these kings that were being prayed for believed. Rather, they are law-abiding citizens, wanting to "live peaceful and quiet lives." The text also applies these civic concerns in the larger context of evangelism, of God's overriding love for the whole world and His desire that His salvation, won at such a cost, be extended to everyone, kings included.

CITIZENSHIP IN AN AGE OF TERRORISM

It is thus fitting that Americans, in their vocations as citizens, rally around their country in time of war. Patriotism is laudable in Christian citizens. The unity one feels with fellow citizens—no matter their religion—is also appropriate.

Notice how so many of the nations plagued by terrorism—Northern Ireland, the former Yugoslavia,

Somalia, India, Israel—are filled with people who identify themselves and each other on the basis of their ethnic group or, more explosively, their religion. They have little sense of a common citizenship, no overarching allegiance to the country to which they all belong. Each group, in the name of its tribe or its religion, seeks to overthrow the rival groups, often refusing to acknowledge or submit to the governing authorities, if they are led by a faction not their own. Christians, by contrast, have a calling to be good citizens wherever they have been placed by God.

Christians can be both patriotic and, when necessary, critical of their government. They are to submit to the lawful authorities and, when necessary, exercise their office of citizenship by voting them out of office. In a time of terrorism and war, they can support their nation's efforts to protect their fellow citizens and to exact retribution against its enemies. But good citizens need to be vigilant, not only against the threat of terrorism, but against the threat of bad government.

In the new cultural climate after 9-11, we must continually assess the political climate as the years unfold. Could the culture go from the extreme of anything goes, the extreme permissiveness that characterized postmodernism, to the other extreme of social oppression? The government's initial responses to the terrorist threat have surely been appropriate. Having to be physically frisked in airports, though, like criminals caught in the act, rubs Americans the wrong way. Such indignities are minor, but what might lie ahead?

Left-wing politicians are rejoicing that the era of distrust of government is over. Whereas the Bible assigns the government one major task, namely, to restrain evil and to punish evildoers (Romans 13: 3–4)—which it is now fulfilling, while arguably neglecting this task before—this may become a pretext for assuming control over many other spheres of life, which are properly the business of other vocations. Many in the timorous public seem willing to give up freedom for security—just as the great Christian cultural critic Francis Schaeffer warned decades ago.[7]

Whatever happens, Christians must not surrender their say in these matters or allow themselves to be silenced just because their concerns (about the terrorism of abortion, for example) are motivated by their Christian faith. This would be to abandon one of their divine callings.

Notes to Chapter 6

1. Richard Niebuhr, *Christ and Culture* (New York: Harper Collins, 1986). See also Angus Menuge, ed., *Christ and Culture in Dialogue* (St. Louis: Concordia Publishing House, 1999).

2. Another option cited by Niebuhr, which is, indeed, the option he prefers, is Christ transforming culture. But this seems to be essentially a variation of Christ above culture.

3. See C. S. Lewis, *The Abolition of Man* (San Francisco: Harper, 2001), particularly the appendix, which compares the moral codes of various cultures and religions.

4. For documentation of this point, as far back as the Middle Ages and before, see E. Stanton Evans, *The Theme Is Freedom: Religion, Politics, and the American Tradition* (Washington, DC: Regnery, 1994).

5. The issues first arose in seventeenth-century England, when Puritans were persecuted for "unlicensed" preaching and for

publishing pamphlets critical of the state church and of the royal government that mandated particular religious beliefs. Such persecution is what brought many of the descendents of the American founders to the New World. Puritans such as John Milton were the first and most forceful advocates of freedom of speech and of the press. See Milton's classic essay "Areopagitica."

6. Kolb, Robert and Timothy J. Wengert, eds. *The Book of Concord* (Minneapolis: Fortress Press, 2000), p. 51.

7. Francis Schaeffer, *How Should We Then Live?* (Old Tappan, NJ: Fleming H. Revell, 1976), pp. 205, 227.

7

WARS AND RUMORS OF WARS

There is no more dramatic manifestation of our fallen condition than war. We live in a world of conflict, not just between individuals but between nations and ideologies and religions. People kill each other, not in the passion of an individual crime, but in an organized, systematic way. Killing in warfare, unlike murder, is "nothing personal." The combatants seldom even know each other and may well be friends if they meet away from the battlefield. Combat can be brutal, traumatic, and nightmarish. And yet it can also be heroic, thrilling, and exhilarating.

One of the dirty little secrets of human history is that, for the most part, the human race loves war. It is certainly part and parcel of most cultures and most civilizations—tribal societies are often organized around its warriors; the history of Western civilization tends to be defined around its wars (from the conquests of Alexander and the rise of the Roman Empire to World War I, World War II, Korea, Vietnam).

War has been pretty much a constant in history, and yet the United States has enjoyed such peace and security that we had forgotten what it is like to be in a state of war. Many of us have become semipacifists, especially those who lived through the war in Vietnam, which became for many a symbol of war's absurdity.

But on September 11, 2001, our nation was attacked. More were killed in the World Trade Center, the Pentagon, and the hijacked aircraft than in Pearl Harbor. Our mainland had not been attacked since the war of 1812. We had always been protected by the vast moats of the oceans from foreign invaders or bombers—and now the security we had taken for granted was lost, maybe forever.

And if this is war, it is a very different kind of war. Not massed army against massed army, but civilians targeting civilians. Warfare is now decentralized. Tiny cells of terrorists operate independently, yet have a global reach, buying airline tickets enabling them to travel anywhere in the world, coordinating their schemes via e-mail. Though few in number, technology makes them lethal—commandeering jumbo jets, blending fuel oil and fertilizer to make an explosive powerful enough to level an office building carried in the back of a rental truck, engineering poisonous gas or a plague of deadly disease and spreading it with a crop duster or a building's ventilation system. A handful of terrorists could kill millions if they could get their hands on a nuclear bomb, as they are trying earnestly to do.

Against this threat the United States has mobilized, with the military counterattacking the terrorists and the states that support them. Technology makes our military both lethal and precise. Bombs guided by global positioning coordinates seldom miss their targets (and, unlike the terrorists, make a point of sparing civilians). Daisy cutters, on the other hand, are bombs the size of a minivan, which obliterate everything within a hundred-yard radius, snapping trees like the stems of flowers. Stealth bombers, invisible to radar, fly all the way to Afghanistan from Missouri. Unmanned Predator surveillance drones, armed with Hellfire missiles, are controlled from Tampa, Florida.

This is a different kind of war, spread out over the whole world, diffuse, with no clear battle lines, little territory to attack and defend, and no clear end in sight. And yet what the human race has learned from its long and bloody history of warfare still pertains. And the moral and spiritual issues raised by war have not changed.

Just War

Christianity is pretty much the only religion that sees war as in any way problematic. The paganism of ancient civilizations treated war as its life's blood. The key Hindu scripture, the *Bhagavad Gita,* hinges on a warrior giving up his qualms about slaughtering his opponents in an unjust war, as the god Krishna urges him to plunge into the fray to fulfill his caste obligations and to recognize the illusory quality of all life. Buddhism addresses suffering not so much by mitigating it but by detaching the consciousness away from it, a stance that allows for both passive endurance and the martial arts of the samurai. As for Islam, holy wars have always been a prime means of spreading the faith.

Christianity, though, has always treasured peace, has urged love even for one's enemy, and has promoted nonviolence. Many Christians in the early church and today—particularly those in the Anabaptist tradition—are pacifists. Military historian Victor Davis Hanson shows in *Culture and Carnage* that as Christians changed from being a persecuted minority to the cultural rulers who had to defend their people against attacks—particularly from Muslim invaders—pacifism gave way to the vocation of Christian warrior.[1]

Though Christians remained morally ambivalent about war, as Hanson shows, the qualms did not prevent them from waging war on a monumentally effective scale. But what they did was to put war, in all of its brutality, under a higher law. Not that they always obeyed their own moral codes, but they tried to distinguish between warfare as tragic necessity, waged by Christians in lawful vocation, and warfare as the unleashing of human sin.

Augustine set forth moral requirements for a just war. In the Middle Ages, the church exercised its authority to regulate combat. This tradition continued in more modern times with treaties to put legal limits on acts of war. These include the Hague Conventions—"Laws and Customs of War on Land"—of 1899 and 1907, and the Geneva Conventions of 1929 and 1949. These were signed by "all civilized nations."

They certainly were not always followed, and they did not prevent the West from practicing what Hanson describes as its unique brand of total, relentless military domination. But these laws of war did distinguish between combatants and noncombatants and set standards for the humane treatment of prisoners. They also at least attempt to apply some moral limits to the intrinsic brutality of warfare. How do these laws apply in an age of terrorism?

According to Augustine, there are five criteria for a "just war." First, the cause must be just. Wars are justified in cases of self-defense and should not be waged for conquest, plunder, or political oppression. Second, a just war must be initiated by a proper authority. Nations with lawful governments, legitimate leadership, and duly organized and disciplined militaries have the authority to wage war. Irregular bands of fighters and unorganized mobs, bent only on plunder and mayhem, are not fighting a just war. They lack the vocation for it. Third, a just war must be fought with the right intention. That is, the purpose of the war should be peace. Waging war out of bad intentions—to slaughter the innocent, to scapegoat an enemy as a political distraction, to seek power for its own sake—is immoral. Fourth, a just war must have a reasonable chance of success. Hopeless causes make people kill and die in vain. A tiny army against the Roman Empire, Augustine would say, would do best to surrender and accept terms rather than fight to the death. Even a powerful army, for various reasons such as political limitations, may not enjoy a reasonable chance of success—think of the Vietnam War. Fifth, a just war must use means proportional to the end. Slaughtering a whole population because of a trade dispute is wildly out of proportion. If the end, the purpose of the war, is to liberate an oppressed people, it makes no sense to bring them under further subjection, nor does using nuclear weapons against guerilla fighters. Unless, of course, they employ nuclear weapons of their own, in which case a nuclear response is proportional.

By these criteria, it is evident that the terrorists of 9-11 were not waging a just war. In fact, they violated every tenet. They did not act justly. They were not acting in self-defense, nor was their motivating cause—Islamic zeal—related to the murders they committed. The terrorists did not possess legitimate legal authority for their attack. No one elected Osama bin Laden, nor did he have any legal standing to order the destruction that he did. In fact, his native Saudi Arabia had previously revoked his citizenship. The members of al Qaeda were not members of an official military force, nor were they under military orders or an authorized chain of command. They were and are "unlawful combatants," civilian killers acting outside of any law. Nor were their intentions proper. Their intent was to kill civilians, to slaughter innocent bystanders who had nothing to do with their cause or their grievances. Nor did they have a reasonable chance of success. Did they think they could conquer the United States and bring its citizens under their control? Nor were their ends (to make a statement against Israel) related in any way to their means (crashing aircraft into buildings).

Conversely, each of the requirements for just war is met in the American response. The cause is just, in fact, one of the few causes that is universally regarded as just: self-defense. The United States was attacked by enemies who desire to kill even more of its citizens. Of course the nation is right to counterattack and to root out those who threaten its security. The American war against terrorism is under lawful authority: the president as commander-in-chief, the congress authorizing military action, the nation's armed services being lawfully mobilized and deployed, the law-enforcement professionals of the police and FBI tracking down terrorist cells. The intention is right. The goal is to create peace and security, not to subjugate Muslims nor to kill innocent civilians. The United States does have a reasonable prospect for success, as seen in the quick overthrow of the Taliban, though the war against terrorism is, by its nature, a disturbingly long-term commitment. The means are proportional to the ends, for the most part. Though it may not seem fair to employ precision, laser-guided bombs and Hellfire missiles against terrorists on horseback, as a response to a disproportional attack that killed thousands of Americans, the use of overwhelming force is appropriate, especially since the precision technology serves to minimize civilian casualties. The indiscriminate scope of the weapons of mass destruction the terrorists prefer, from hijacked airliners to biological and chemical and nuclear weapons, is in stark contrast to the precision weaponry used by the United States, which avoids mass destruction in an attempt to zero in on just those who deserve to be targeted.

And yet, though it can be reasonably proven that the terrorists are waging an unjust war and the United States and its allies are waging a just war, that is not the last word on the matter. Luther warned about relying too much on the justness of one's cause when waging war. Trusting in one's own righteousness is deadly in the spiritual realm, and it can be dangerous in the earthly realm as well. The just-war theory was an integral part of medieval moral philosophy. Luther believed that this approach to morality, under which actions can be justified or condemned by checking off criteria, neglects the radical power of sin, which taints even our good works, and encourages a naive "works-righteousness" that obscures the Gospel. Luther, while not rejecting Augustine's just-war theory, approaches war from a different angle. He condemns with a pacifist's zeal any kind of religious war, while, in light of his doctrine of the two kingdoms and his doctrine of vocation, he sees warfare in light of God's judgment and grace and recognizes the legitimacy of what he called "wars of necessity."

AGAINST HOLY WAR

Luther's view of war is highly relevant in an age of terrorism because in many ways he was addressing a context startlingly like our own. And the differences between his situation and our own only make his insights more arresting. In Luther's day, at the height of the Reformation and its controversies, the West was attacked by Muslims. The Turks of the Ottoman Empire, having conquered most of central Asia and northern Africa, invaded Europe. Soon Eastern Europe—Greece, the birthplace of Western civilization; the Balkans; Hungary—all fell to the sword of Islam. No one could stop the Turkish armies, which were advancing closer and closer to a terrified Western Europe. The various fragmented principalities of Austria and Germany were next for the Turks. Once conquered, the rest of Europe would fall easily.

A major difference between then and now was that the Muslims were arguably stronger, more sophisticated, and culturally more powerful than the Christian West. This was the "golden age" of Islam, the era today's Muslims hearken back to as the pinnacle of their glory. The Muslims then led the world in science, mathematics, and medicine. In fact, Islamic scholars had preserved many classic writings in Greek and Latin—texts which, when brought back to the West, precipitated the Renaissance. This golden era of Islam, which actually stretches back through the Middle Ages, is what Muslim apologists today point to for the great cultural contributions and enlightened tolerance of true Islam. In turn, the memories of this past glory embitter today's Muslims. They have been culturally and technologically eclipsed by the West—something that should have been impossible, given the truth of Islam and the divine culture imposed by the Qur'an. They regard the success of infidel Europe, Israel, and America as an intrinsic injustice, comprehensible only in terms of a dark, satanic plot.

The Ottomans ruled over a vast and diverse empire and in many ways were enlightened. Though they showed signs of "tolerance" toward Christians and Jews—they let them operate in autonomous but strictly supervised spheres, rigorously segregated from the rest of society—they also practiced a peculiar mode of forced conversion and slavery. The emperor was entitled to one-fifth of all war plunder. This was construed to include a share of the captives and the defeated population. These became his personal slaves. By forcing them to convert to Islam and raising them into a warrior caste, he developed an elite slave army, the Janissaries. To man the vast imperial bureaucracy, the Ottomans would identify promising children among the Christians and then take them away from their parents, raise them as Muslims, and make them the emperor's slaves. They were, however, very powerful slaves, running the empire and controlling vast holdings. Since they were his personal property, these so-called *devshirme* exercised the emperor's authority and kept everything under his control. In the sixteenth century the Turkish Emperor Süleyman the Magnificent—the name adopted by his American fan, the al Qaeda volunteer John Walker Lindh—moved to spread his system and his faith into the West.

The Christian Emperor, Charles V, had nothing like Süleyman's power. His family, the Hapsburgs, held the hereditary title of Holy Roman Emperor, but this mainly amounted to dominions in Spain, Italy, Austria, and Hungary, plus vassals who owed him allegiance in Germany and elsewhere. But whereas the Ottoman Emperor ruled absolutely, claiming the whole empire as his personal property and holding all of his vassals, officials, armies, and even his ruling lords as his slaves, the European emperor was under the law. His vassals and the lesser nobility had rights of their own. In fact, the emperor had to be elected. A specific group of nobles inherited the right to vote for and thus to choose the Holy Roman Emperor. Among these was the Elector Frederick, Duke of Saxony, who became Luther's patron and protector.

For Charles V, the Reformation came at the worst possible time. Why get embroiled in all of these theological controversies when the fate of Christendom itself was at stake? Surely this was the time to unite against a common foe, not separate into factions at war with each other. The religious feelings were so high that military cooperation, on the part of the various nobles, was proving impossible, even when the common foe was at the gates. In fact many scholars believe that the fall of Hungary to the Turks was largely due to the discord between the Reformation Hungarians and the Catholic Hungarians, so that all Süleyman had to do to this already divided nation was to conquer. The Holy Roman Emperor would have burned Luther at the stake, but Duke Frederick—*Elector* Frederick—who had adopted his cause, was too powerful to defy. And now, even the advocates of the Reformation were splintering, with Lutherans and the Reformed refusing to get along with each other. Surely, the emperor felt, all of this theological squabbling should be set aside in order to deal with the much more important priority of saving Europe from the Turks.

The pope, of course, agreed. He proclaimed a

Crusade, complete with indulgences for those who fight and die to defend the true faith. He called on all Christians to unite under the emperor to repel the Turk in a Holy War. Fighting the Muslims was a religious duty, a Christian act. It was up to the emperor to defend Christianity. Both pope and emperor agreed that the Turkish invasion was a religious war and that the survival of Christianity hinged on their victory.

Luther, to their consternation, disagreed. In answering the papal bull, which among other things accused him of undermining the war against the Turks, Luther made clear that his objection was to spiritualizing the war, especially in turning it into a Crusade, with indulgences and promises that fighting the Turks can be awarded by salvation. "We should not plunge into war, relying on the pope's indulgence, with which he has deceived Christians in the past and is deceiving them still," Luther said, in his answer to the papal bull (1521). "All the pope accomplishes with his crusading indulgences and his promises of heaven is to lead Christians with their lives into death and with their souls into hell. . . . God does not demand crusades, indulgences, and wars."[2]

In a treatise that directly addressed the issue, "On War Against the Turk" (1529), Luther insisted that it is not up to human beings to defend God:

> The urging and inciting with which the emperor and the princes have been stirred up to fight against the Turk ought to cease. He has been urged, as head of Christendom and as protector of the church and defender of the faith, to wipe out the Turk's religion, and the urging and

exhorting have been based on the wickedness and vice of the Turks. Not so! The emperor is not the head of Christendom or defender of the gospel or the faith. The church and the faith must have a defender other than emperor and kings.[3]

Nor should the purpose of the war be directed against a particular religion. "And if the emperor were supposed to destroy the unbelievers and non-Christians, he would have to begin with the pope, bishops, and clergy, and perhaps not spare us or himself; for there is enough horrible idolatry in his own empire to make it unnecessary for him to fight the Turks for this reason. . . . Let the Turk believe and live as he will."[4]

There is no such thing, Luther believed, as a Holy War, whether a Crusade or a jihad. There *is* a reason to fight the Turks, but it is not to defend Christianity— God can handle that—nor to punish nonbelievers. As always with Luther, Christianity has to do not with what *we* do, but what *God* does. We can leave the spiritual issues in His hands. War has to do with our earthly lives, and the authority to wage war has to do with earthly vocations.

"The emperor's sword has nothing to do with the faith," said Luther; "it belongs to physical, worldly things." A crusade, an earthly war for a spiritual cause, confuses the two kingdoms. The emperor wields the sword; the church wields the Word. Faith is never to be a matter of force, coercion, or violence. War has to do with the secular kingdom, and the emperor, because of his calling, has the authority to wage war in secular terms:

> The emperor should seek nothing else than simply to perform the work and duty of his office, which is to protect his subjects; and those under his banner should seek simply to do the work and duty of obedience. If there is to be war against the Turk, it should be fought at the emperor's command, under his banner, and in his name. Then everyone can be sure in his conscience that he is obeying the ordinance of God, since we know that the emperor is our true overlord and head and that whoever obeys him in such a case obeys God also, whereas he who disobeys him also disobeys God. If he dies in this obedience, he dies in a good state, and if he has previously repented and believes in Christ, he will be saved.[5]

God does rule in His earthly kingdom, working through the lawful magistrates to restrain evil (Romans 13). Ruling and fighting are matters of vocation. But they are never to be confused with spiritual issues. They can never merit salvation nor advance the cause of Christ. While abjuring the idea of a holy war, Luther did recognize the impending threat and in 1529 encouraged Protestant troops to help defend Vienna. Here, the Turks were defeated. Christian Europe was saved from Islamic conquest after all.

War of Necessity

The main function of earthly government, according to Romans 13, is to protect its subjects and to punish evil. In a sinful world, this often entails using force and "bearing the sword." Just as an earthly ruler has the right to use force within his borders, Luther believed that he has the right to use force outside his borders when this is necessary for the biblical mandate to protect his people.[6]

The only legitimate war, therefore, according to Luther, is a defensive war. Paul Althaus summarizes Luther's teachings about war:

> Implicit in what Luther says is that he recognizes only a defensive war which is forced upon us by an aggressor. War is right only when it is "our only miserable way of defending ourselves." Luther knows that most wars are waged for quite different reason: selfish motives of princes and lords, lust for the property and possessions of others, desire for glory, the feeling that our honor has been insulted, wrath, and the desire for revenge. However, a Christian prince is forbidden to wage war for such reasons. The one and only purpose of a war must be to protect his subjects against attack. In this sense the decision to go to war and the decisions about how war is to be waged must be quite "simple."[7]

Thus, according to Luther in one of his breathtakingly simple, yet profound, generalizations, "Whoever starts a war is in the wrong."[8]

Those who start the war are wrong, but those who have been attacked are engaged in what Luther called a "war of necessity." This kind of war is in contrast to those launched intentionally and deliberately, which he described as being from the devil. A war of necessity, though, is a "human accident, in which we can expect God's help." The prince must wage this necessary war "joyfully and with a good conscience," decisively, energetically, and with the confidence that he is within God's will.[9]

Luther actually goes beyond just-war theory, with even stricter principles against what can justify warfare. His point, though, is not to just set up legalistic criteria. Rather, he wants to prevent both rulers and their subjects from trusting in the justice of their cause, as if this will ensure success. As Althaus summarizes:

> Anyone who trusts in his own cause and his own power is foolhardy. As seriously as Luther admonishes a prince to do his duty in a specific instance and to use his weapons to protect his subjects, and as strongly as he emphasizes the prince's responsibility for his country, he in no way creates the expectation that the prince whose "cause is just" will win. Luther says to the prince: Because your whole country is threatened, you must take the risk and see whether God wants to help you. Luther speaks of risk because no one knows how the conflict will end. Even the fact that one has been attacked and has good reason to defend himself does not guarantee his success. It is of no use to emphasize the justice of one's cause, for this, like all pride, stubbornness, and security, is an abomination to God. We ought not to rely on the justice of our cause, only on God's grace and mercy.[10]

In war, as in every other facet of life, we remain under the cross and we are utterly dependent on the grace of God.

WAR AND VOCATION

One of Luther's key writings on vocation was a pamphlet entitled *Whether Soldiers Too Can Be Saved* (1526). Many Christians, in the first Reformation flush of rediscovering the Bible, maintained that since we are supposed to love our enemies, Christians may not serve in the military. Soldiers must kill. Since we are supposed to forgive sinners, Christians may not serve as magistrates. Judges must punish.

In response, Luther asked whether God is allowed to take a human life or to punish sin. Indeed, He is. It is God, working through the offices of judge or soldier, who takes life and punishes sin. Christians can indeed occupy these offices—to be called to them as divine vocations—so that a soldier is loving his neighbor when he protects his country; a judge is loving his neighbor when he puts a criminal in prison or delivers him over to the hangman (another valid Christian vocation).

This by no means negates the commands to love our enemies and to forgive those who trespass against us. In their private life, soldiers, judges, and hangmen must indeed love and forgive. But in their vocations, by virtue of their offices, they are authorized to "bear the sword."

Not that this authorization is unconditional. Vocation, as in every aspect of God's secular kingdom, remains under the moral Law. Those who use their office to disobey God are violating their calling and no longer bear His authority. In the case of a ruler who wages an unjust war—that is, one that is not defensive—Luther goes so far as to recommend that soldiers refuse to obey, desert their stations, and save their souls.[11]

And yet, being a soldier is a valid and praiseworthy vocation. A soldier risks his life for his neighbor and thus, even when he must kill, he acts in faith and love. Luther even wrote a "soldier's prayer." It encapsulates and applies, practically and in a life-and-death situation, the distinction between Law and Gospel, the two kingdoms and the doctrine of vocation, the theology of the cross, and dependence on the will and the grace of God. A modernized version is included in the *Service Hymnal* used by military chaplains, to be prayed before going into battle:

> Dear God, You know that I must now go into combat. You know that I would rather keep out of it, but that this is no longer possible. O heavenly Father, because You have placed me here in this duty, I know that it is God-pleasing. I know that You have called me to serve my nation. My first loyalty is to You; then to my country, for Your sake. I thank You that You have graciously called me to this honorable work, to protect and preserve life, if need be even by fighting. I know that this is not sinful, but righteous and obedient according to Your will. I have learned from Your Word that our works cannot save us; neither can military service. So I will not put my trust in our righteous cause, but in Your grace. I will not rely on my mission to earn me heaven, but I will perform this duty as a service to Your will. Enable me to believe with all my heart that only the innocent blood of Your dear Son, my Lord Jesus

Christ, obediently shed for me according to Your gracious will, can redeem and save me. In this faith, Lord, I will go forward, wage war, do all that has to do with war, and if need be die. Dear God and Father, preserve and strengthen this faith in me through Your Holy Spirit. Into Your hands I commend my body and soul. Amen![12]

Notes to Chapter 7

1. Victor Davis Hanson, *Culture and Carnage* (New York: Doubleday, 2001).

2. Luther, "Defense and Explanation of All the Articles," 32:90.

3. Luther, "On War Against the Turk," 46:184.

4. Ibid.

5. Ibid.

6. Paul Althaus, *The Ethics of Martin Luther* (Philadelphia: Fortress Press, 1972), p. 137.

7. Ibid., p. 138.

8. Luther, "Whether Soldiers Too Can Be Saved," 46:117

9. Althaus, *Ethics of Martin Luther*, p. 139, quoting "Whether Soldiers Too Can Be Saved," 46:120.

10. Althaus, *Ethics of Martin Luther*, p. 140.

11. Althaus, *Ethics of Martin Luther*, p. 127. See Luther, "Whether Soldiers Too Can Be Saved," 46:130, and "Treatise on Good Works," 44:100.

12. *Service Hymnal* (St. Louis: Concordia Publishing House, 1993).

8

THE NEW CULTURAL CLIMATE

When an enemy assaulted their country, Americans suddenly got serious. The latest vile reality TV show, "Love Cruise: The Maiden Voyage," was all set to premier that Tuesday night, but it was pre-empted by a real reality show, the news accounts of what happened in New York City and Washington, D.C. The Emmy Awards, television's love fest with itself, was cancelled, even though it was not going to happen until Sunday. "This is a national crisis," Emmy producer Don Mischer told *Variety*, "and no time to be handing out awards or to comment on what people are wearing." There was no Jay Leno monologue, no Letterman Top Ten list, as both late-night talk shows were cancelled. No one was in the mood for political humor.

Across the nation, movie theaters shut down, as did shopping malls, theme parks, and even casinos. Major-league baseball cancelled games, something that happened only three other times in history (the deaths of Presidents Warren G. Harding and Franklin Delano Roosevelt, and D-Day). Other sports, from the PGA to NASCAR to the NFL, cancelled their events. It was not because there was any particular security threat to stadiums, cineplexes, or malls, but just because it didn't seem right to play when New York City burned.

Cable and satellite television have given Americans hundreds of entertainment channels. But on that Tuesday night, the multiplicity of networks zeroed in on the one topic on everyone's mind. American viewers were brought together in a collective television experience unknown since the days when there were only three networks.

With just a few exceptions, the various channels suspended their regularly scheduled programming to show, over and over again, that plane slamming into the World Trade Center, the Pentagon smoldering, the ordinary folks who had been targeted, the analysts trying to figure out what had happened.

Channels such as the Food Network, Home and Garden, and Direct Sports posted a notice: "Due to today's tragic events, this channel will not be seen today. Our thoughts go out to the victims and their families." Others, including the Home Shopping Network, Country Music Television, and even the usually trivial and escapist MTV played the feed from CNN, Fox News, or a Big Three news affiliate.

Even the Internet, slowed by the millions of people surfing for information, contributed to the unifying media experience. On AOL just about every channel, including Entertainment and Sports, had a box giving the news updates. On Amazon.com, the usual advertisements on the welcome page were replaced by a sober black and white box, expressing sorrow for what happened and offering a point-and-click way to contribute money to the Red Cross Disaster Fund.

Though Americans turned away from their fantasy worlds for that one night, the reality of what happened seemed like a fiction, an "unbelievable" event as in one of those techno-thriller novels, which have terrorists hijacking an aircraft carrier or something equally implausible. The news accounts, with the apparently well-organized and perfectly executed terrorist conspiracy, were going beyond Tom Clancy novels.

Indeed, Tom Clancy was a guest on CNN, one of the many experts being interviewed to help viewers make sense of the catastrophe. Obviously, Judy Woodruff, who conducted the interview, had never read Clancy's novels, otherwise she would not have ignored the major reason to have him on the air. Two of his novels, *Debt of Honor* and *Executive Orders*, hinge on an airliner being used as a terrorist weapon when it is crashed into the U.S. Capitol building. She should have asked him, could the terrorists have been Tom Clancy fans? It used to be that fiction imitated reality. Now, it seemed that reality was imitating fiction.

At the same time, the horrific events of September 11 brought Americans, long complacent by their peace and prosperity, into facing the bigger realities, including the imminent possibility of death, the true insecurity of this life, and the depths of human sinfulness that could do such a thing. Other, nearly comatose emotions started to stir in Americans' hearts: patriotism, righteous anger, and the primal call to war.

All of a sudden, though Americans lost their taste for the shallow pleasures manufactured by the entertainment industry, the authentic currents of their civilization—what their ancestors fought and died for—were thrown into high relief. Watching movies, reading books, and watching TV shows like "The Band of Brothers," all about the "greatest generation" that fought World War II, happened to be all the rage. Now, those principles they were fighting for in the 1940s, and the carnage that accompanied the fight, become an issue for the present generation.

The old books, the old ideas, and the old theologies became relevant again in the way the confections of the pop culture could never be. My own vocation is that of an English professor. The morning of the attack, I had an English Lit class. The students were glued to the classroom TV monitor when I came in, and together we watched the first tower fall. But after awhile, out of some vocational duty, I turned off the television and we resumed our discussion of *Beowulf*.

That ancient epic depicts the construction of a great building called "Heorot," the biggest and most magnificent mead hall in the world, in which the tribe of the Shieldings feasted, celebrated, and enjoyed their prosperity. But for all of their joy, success, and security, they could not keep out the Monster. Grendel, a descendent of Cain, intrudes on their cultural complacency, breaks into their great mead hall, and ravenously murders scores of great warriors as they sleep. The parallels of Heorot and the World Trade Center, as the class analyzed this ancient poem, were chilling. So was what happened next. Beowulf killed Grendel, but he and the Shieldings became caught up in a bloodbath of revenge and constantly escalating retributions.

Grendel and the rest of the monsters were symbols for the mystery of iniquity that has a way of interrupting every period of happiness and spoiling every civilization. Optimistic Americans tend to forget about the monsters lurking in the dark, something Christians and now the rest of America know are real.

REPENTANCE

Jesus Himself was asked about the meaning of atrocities and the falling of towers, who is to blame and what our response should be:

> Now there were some present at that time who told Jesus about the Galileans whose blood Pilate had mixed with their sacrifices. Jesus answered, "Do you think that these Galileans were worse sinners than all the other Galileans because they suffered this way? I tell you, no! But unless you repent, you too will all perish. Or those eighteen who died when the tower in Siloam fell on them—do you think they were more guilty than all the others living in Jerusalem? I tell you, no! But unless you repent, you too will all perish." (Luke 13:1–5)

The victims of Pilate's cruelty and the catastrophe at Siloam were *not* being punished for their sins. And yet, such horrible tragedies should inspire the rest of us, the survivors, to repentance.

This was Luther's point, too, when he acknowledged the right of the emperor and the princes to protect their people from the Turk and yet insisted that first the people being attacked should repent of their sins. The part of the emperor and his military forces is indeed to fight against the Turkish assault, in God's secular kingdom. The part of the Christian, in God's spiritual kingdom, is to repent and pray.

> I have wanted to tell all this to the . . . Christian, so that he may know and see how much need there is for prayer, and how he must first smite the Turk's Allah, that is, his god the devil, and overcome his power and divinity; otherwise, I fear, the sword will accomplish little. Now this man is not to fight physically with the Turk, as the pope and his followers teach; nor is he to resist the Turk with the fist, but he is to recognize the Turk as God's rod and wrath which Christians must either suffer, if God visits their sins upon them, or fight against and drive away with repentance, tears, and prayer.[1]

The Turk, even though serving the devil, is to be understood as God's rod, His means of punishing sin. Even though those being invaded are the victims of an evil power, they are to fight against it with spiritual means, by repenting of their sins and turning to God in prayer.

Christians operating in the spiritual kingdom may fight only with the Word of God and with prayer, but Christians have a simultaneous vocation in God's earthly kingdom, and here they are indeed to oppose the Turk with the sword. "The . . . man who ought to fight against the Turk is Emperor Charles, or whoever may be emperor; for the Turk is attacking his subjects and his empire, and it is his duty, as a regular ruler appointed by God, to defend his own."[2] But apart from repentance and prayer, Luther believed, the sword will be futile. "The Turk is such a mighty lord that no kingdom or land, whatever it is, is strong enough to resist him alone, unless God performs a miracle."[3] Therefore, he concludes, "I would not urge or bid anyone to fight against the Turk unless the first method, mentioned above, that men had first repented and been reconciled to God, etc., had been followed. If anyone wants to go to war in another way, let him take his chances."[4]

As Paul Althaus, in *The Ethics of Martin Luther*, explains, Luther recognized that the Turks threatened Christianity, and yet, "at the same time he recognized that God was using them to discipline Christendom and that Christendom ought to respond to such discipline in a Christian way, that is, with repentance and prayer."[5] The two kingdoms, however, work together, carrying on the conflict in different ways. "Christendom with the weapons of repentance, conversion, and prayer; the emperor with his military power."[6]

> But Luther concludes that military power alone will hardly be very effective against the Turks. For the Turk who is an enemy of Christ is at the same time God's instrument of discipline, and behind his power stands the devil. This theological dimension of the secular and political opposition between the empire and the Turks must be

recognized. It means that only repentance, conversion, and prayer—not military force—have the power "to take the rod out of God's hand, so that the Turk may be found only, in his own strength, all by himself, without the devil's help and without God's hand."[7]

LIVING WITH TERRORISM

How does this relate to our situation today? Surely the United States, its citizens targeted in an unprovoked attack, is waging a "war of necessity," indeed, a "just war." And yet, we have much to repent for. Every kind of catastrophe, every horrible accident and crime, reminds us of the fragility of our lives, taking away our security by which we deny the certain prospect of death. Facing death and the ever present possibility of death speaks to us of Law, the inescapable reality of sin, and the wages of sin.

The uneasy climate of the age of terrorism, the realization that an attack or a bombing or a biological weapon could be imminent at any time, makes it less easy to enjoy complacency, that great obstacle to the faith. Living in the knowledge of death and the knowledge of sin in the world, including our own, can drive people to the grace of God in Christ.

Christianity has to do with the Gospel, and Christians must beware of lurching from complacent immorality to the other extreme of a new self-righteous legalism. We are not saved by our good works, and those who think they are—such is the power of sin—tend to actually perform *bad works*. Thus, the ter-

rorists claim allegiance to the most moralistic of religions, which they use as a pretext to commit the most
brutal atrocities. Christians must not play that game.

Some today think that all religions of the world
are the same; that is to say, equally good. Others agree
that they are the same, but conclude that they are
equally bad. Perhaps Christians, who believe in the
Gospel, should agree with the secularists: The world's
religions are all wrong, insofar as they result in self-
righteousness, self-divinization, and a seared conscience that justifies wickedness in the name of its false
gods.

The Gospel, in contrast, puts its trust in God's
action, not our own, trading sin for forgiveness, hate
for love, and glory for the cross. In an age of terrorism,
Jesus Christ is the only security anyone can have.

Notes to Chapter 8
  1. Luther, "On War Against the Turk," 46:184.
  2. Ibid.
  3. Ibid.
  4. Ibid.
  5. Paul Althaus, *Ethics of Martin Luther*, p. 142.
  6. Ibid.
  7. Ibid.